RECRUIT
YOUR WAY TO
— 6 —
FIGURE$

TOP EARNERS RECRUITING SECRETS
NETWORK MARKETING

TGON Publishing

TGON Publishing

ISBN 978-1-7343817-3-3

CONTENTS

INTRODUCTION

I have a passion for helping people in network marketing find success. It`s something I`ve been doing for decades.

In fact, I was the number one recruiter out of a million distributors! Hard to believe that this accomplishment could come from an absolute introvert! But there is something you should know. You can learn how to recruit. I had to learn how to sell. I had to learn how to network. I had to learn how to recruit. Recruiting is a skill that everyone needs to learn in order to find success in network marketing.

I have since retired from network marketing, and now have the opportunity to coach and help network marketing businesses and people around the world. The best part of my job is being able to help people from any network marketing company learn the skills to create success in this business. One of the questions I get asked the most is, "How do you recruit?"

Currently, I`m running several mastermind groups that focus on helping others take their businesses to the next level. At one of my last events, I had over 29 six to seven figure earners come together to learn and collaborate together.

The greatest part about masterminds is even though I am there to teach, I learn so much from the incredible people in the room. The knowledge, experience, and expertise are mind blowing. As I sat and listened to these highly successful people talk about their success and their processes, I kept thinking how much value this group was sharing. I wanted everyone in network marketing to be in that room and be able to learn from these incredible individuals.

This book is the closest thing I could come to getting you all in the room at our mastermind event! I have taken my expert coaching, combined it with these highly successful network marketers, and brought you the best book on recruiting there is right now in network marketing. The book is jam-packed with how to take your business to the next level in recruiting. There are actions that you can take today with specific strategies to help shift the momentum of your business.

Many of you may have read my book *The Game of Conquering* where I went into depth about the main fears people face in network marketing. I had several of you reach out and say, "I can overcome my fears, but then what? Where do I go next?"

This is the perfect book to make you more confident in your recruiting skills. Becoming a great recruiter starts with something simple. It all starts with "I am." What are you telling yourself? How do you see yourself?

Are you saying, "I am a terrible recruiter, I am in a bad area, I am not experienced enough?" That is going to get you nowhere! In fact, let`s replace it with a simple switch, "I am learning. I am growing. I am becoming a great recruiter." It really does start right here.

You have to give your mind something to focus on. Your brain can`t hold the problem and the solution at the same time. It just can`t!

If you want to learn more about the power of mindset, along with a couple more tips about recruiting, check out this website, www.Sperrybonus.com.

As you keep reading this book, think of some "I am" statements that are going to help you. Here are a couple to get you started.

"I am learning from the best."
"I am going to use these tools in my business today."
"I am going to find motivation in the stories shared."
"I am going to be an author in one of Rob`s books myself!"

I want to make sure that you aren`t going to be an "askhole!" Don`t be the person that is only asking for advice and not taking advantage of the advice given. As you read this book, think about the recommended information I provide for your business. Don`t be an "askhole," be an "implementer!" The authors and I are investing in you to become the best you can be.

Let me tell how this book is set up. I interviewed and hand-selected some of the top leaders in the industry. Each one of them is very well known in network marketing and has proven his or her. As you read, look at the bio section that starts each chapter. The stats and accomplishments of these people is astounding!

Their accomplishments range from being multi-million-dollar earners to growing diverse teams around the globe, and the list goes on! People pay thousands to see these authors speak and give insight into their recruiting success.

I am honored that each of them said yes to sharing their knowledge in this book. Furthermore, each of the authors have selected their own topics about recruiting. This book is filled with the biggest influencers sharing their expertise in recruiting. Their stories will help you grow your business.

In each chapter you will also find "Rob`s notes." This is my personal feedback about the topics each author shares. We can all find tips, techniques, and stories to inspire us to grow and become the next version of ourselves. Get ready to learn your next recruiting strategy from some of the best in network marketing.

Author: Rachel Pekarek

- Founder of Team Heart and our Master Pro 10 support leader.

- College dropout who lives in Minneapolis MN with her husband Tony and her adorable fur babies Oakley and Sugar.

- Started in her first Network Marketing venture when she was 21 years old and failed forward for several years until finding the right mentor and system to succeed with.

- Over the last 8 years earned over $5 million working from home.

- Leads teams of over 300,000 consumers starting a wellness journey.

- Helped over 100 people reach six or seven figures and thousands more make a "comma" check every single month.

- Actively working with organizations to build orphanages and homes in third world countries like Belize and Nicaragua.

- Her number one focus is to bring raising awareness and rehabilitation for youth trapped in human / sex trafficking.

"Work harder on yourself than you do on your business and you'll be unusually successful."

-Jim Rohn

You're Pretty Bad at This

I sat there pretty shell-shocked. I joined my first network marketing company as a 21-year old college dropout. My sponsor sat across the table seemingly unimpressed by my total enrollments in the first thirty days of my business. Spoiler alert: I signed up zero people!

He said, "You are pretty bad at this."

He was right. I was pretty bad. Reality check, I was really bad. But, I did have one thing. I was committed, and willing to learn.

My sponsor could see that commitment and willingness in me and decided I was worth investing his time in. He shoved a bunch of books and tapes across the table and said, "Rachel, read these. Listen to these." And I did.

I joined this industry as a solution. I was working 50 plus hours a week for a bipolar boss, commuting two and a half hours a day and I was totally miserable.

Although I was skeptical when I attended my first network marketing event, I saw the big picture; the picture of leverage. The idea that you could build and drive a service through a network made sense to me. I saw the vision and it opened my mind to the possibility of what this business could look like for me. Do you remember when you saw your first real vision?

Despite how bad I was starting off, I knew I could learn any skill when I put my mind to it. My two-and-a-half-hour commute became like "Automobile University." As a result, I became ravenous with consuming all network marketing knowledge.

My "warm market", or the people I knew, quickly filled up my pipeline in my first month. By month two I created a newfound belief that I could make this happen. I enrolled 12 people, and soon after I was making enough per week to quit my job.

For many years with my first network marketing company, my earnings were flat-lined. I love network marketing and knew the business model was amazing. I went and found the right business, the right product, the right system and most importantly - the right mentor. I was able to transform from a network marketing amateur to a professional earning a couple thousand dollars a month to over $5.5 million dollars in the last 8 years.

Friends First

One of the biggest mistakes network marketers make is we forget that it`s network marketing! In order to thrive in this business, you have to develop a solid widespread network. It`s not about who you know, but how many people know, like, and trust you.

I developed a "friends first" philosophy. This helps to create the mindset that, "I`m a professional networker." Before I engage in talking about the product, I become friends first with everyone. I`m proud to say that in every major city, I met many wonderful people and cultivated friendships with them. I have stayed at their house, met them for coffee or lunch, and have engaged them in any possible way.

With building friendships all over the world, this philosophy served me well both personally and professionally. Why? Because when people know how much you genuinely care and don`t see you as completely self-serving, they are more open to doing business with you, or send you referrals.

All of my friends know what I do, they`ve seen the products and the business plan. I don`t care if they join, but I do care that they at least take a look. They know if they ever want to join me in business, I will still be here for them as a friend. Nothing changes the fact that friends come first.

I never want it to be weird with my friends. Wouldn`t you hate that? To see your friend at the grocery store who was on your zoom opportunity meeting last week? You think to yourself, "do I bring it up or are they going to?" They are probably wondering, "should I say something? Are they going to ask me?" Set the expectations upfront.

"Listen Mary, I know this may or may not be for you and it`s totally okay if it isn`t, but I am excited to share your story, your vision and your goals! I`m going to the top with this! Regardless whether you join, it will not change anything between you and me. Capiche?"

Assertive? You`re darn right, but I want our friendship to be the focus. It will take away the feeling of a "just direct sales approach" that everyone hates.

In order to be a good friend, you need to be good at the art of people. Learn how to study people. I had an uncle who was a high-powered CEO for a Microsoft brand. He was disappointed I got involved in network marketing, but nonetheless, he gave me excellent advice. "Learn less about your products and more about people. Become an expert in people." My oh my, that has always been golden advice!

If I`m not researching alternative news sources or reading my Bible, then I`m usually studying people. All humans desire to love and to be loved in return. We have a deep, ingrained need to have connections with other like-minded souls.

My approach with my "friends first philosophy" is to love and accept them for who they are but that does not mean being bashful about my company. If you believe in your products, then see the opportunity as a gift.

I want all my friends whom I love dearly to know what I am presenting to them. I do not push, I do not beg, and I do not buy them in. If you have to beg friends to get started, then you`re going to beg them throughout the whole process. In other words, you can lead a thousand, but you can only carry one on your back.

Guide people in their own way, serve them big and be genuinely interested in their life. When you present a business, detach yourself from the choices they make while establishing yourself as their friend.

Rob's Notes: I featured Rachel in my book *The Game of Conquering* for this exact reason. She gets it! Friends first! It is very difficult to become a great recruiter if you become a taker. You won`t feel great about yourself and whether you realize it or not, it will hold you back. Of course, you want everyone buying your products and joining your business, but you want to do it the right way. You want to be bold but open and friendly. Many people are attracted to Rachel`s style of building trust with people because they can see themselves doing the business the way she does. Friends matter, friends first!

Your Marketing Plan

The second biggest mistake network marketers make is forgetting about the kind of industry we are all in. The whole idea is to market to our network. Every brick and mortar shop that is producing a million dollars a year has a marketing plan.

There are too many network marketers that don`t have a plan. It`s crazy to me that some people have a lottery mentality. They hope that their marketing is accomplishing something. Do you hope someone is going to see the lifestyle post on Facebook and sign up? Do you hope that recruits will flood into your downline or take you to the top as their superstar? It`s possible, but the chances are probably 00.001 percent. In other words, if you want to have control of your results, you need an organized marketing plan.

In today`s industry, there are only two ways to market your company. The first, online and second, offline. So, what`s your gig? Are you doing social media, creating flyers, producing mixers, or conducting home meetings?

When you dive into the structure of your business, you need to consistently add into your network or sphere of influence. One of the biggest unspoken truths I see from uplines across the globe is they never tell you that you`re going to blow through your warm market in the first year or first couple of months. Whether it`s six months, or five years from now how, will you continually recruit new prospects into your pipeline? Personally, I have done it 90% online.

I started making YouTube videos in 2008 and that was a huge blessing. No one was doing it back then! I always joked it was just me and the cats videos on YouTube when I started.

Within 18 months of doing consistent weekly videos, I had hundreds of thousands of views, 3,000 subscribers and roughly 10,000 people on my mailing list.

An example of how this helped my business was somewhere on the email list was Lisa from the UK. When I launched the business in 2011, she messaged me asking if I was in England yet. We weren`t, but I told her to hang tight! Two years later, we were opening up in Europe and made an announcement about new territorial expansion! When she responded to my email, she said "still here and open!"

While eight and a half months pregnant and going on maternity leave, Lisa had six months to make the business happen. She had done network marketing prior, and over the course of a few years, she hadn`t even profited $1,000. She was driven to succeed with my simple three-step system. Within her six-month deadline, she became a six-figure earner!

Since 2013, she`s never made less than $100,000 US dollars a year. Today, she`s the number one representative for the company in the United Kingdom. It all started with consistent videos, building an email list, staying in contact, and bringing online leads to Skype conversations. She`s not only a legend but one of my closest friends. I`ve stayed in her home and traveled all across Europe with her. If I had not been a good marketer, I wouldn`t have attracted Lisa to my team.

Four years ago, I got an email from some Australians, including two beautiful ladies Charlotte and Gee, that wanted to join my company. I hopped onto a Zoom call with six of them and heard their goals. They wanted to be leaders in Australia. After the meeting, I launched them online and helped them build their own systems. We did a lot of deep mentoring. Now they are doing over $600,000 a month in volume inside of our organization. They contribute to some of the fastest growing pockets in my business.

Be consistent, do the work and you`ll be amazed at what shows up in your inbox. You can market well, increase your skill, and let others build a massive team that stretches beyond your local city and town.

System Dependent

I`m a big systems person. Our team is not the biggest, but we`ve generated over $150,000,000 in sales. Over time, I found a few key elements to make the journey easier.

First, if I needed to say something in my business more than five times, I would create a tool for it. Ask anybody in my organization. I have power points, PDFs, documents, or videos for just about anything. If you are having to repeat yourself more than five times, save yourself the headache and create a duplicable tool for it.

New team members have so many questions. For example, what do I post on social media? How do I create invites to a launch zoom? What is the current promotion? Make it easy for you and for them by having a system in place to help walk them through the answers to the most asked questions.

Second, you cannot duplicate but you can mobilize. Duplication is a myth. Nobody can be Rob Sperry. I mean, look at his infinite wisdom and rugged good looks. But seriously, he`s a genius. Don`t focus on "duplicating yourself," focus on systems that can help mobilize the newest person for success.

Use simple scripts, tools, copy and paste. Make it easy to share. This will get people moving faster.

Third, it`s important to define your three-step system. In human nature there are one, two, three - OR many steps that you can take. If you get past three steps, it becomes overwhelming to understand. This is our system ITT (Invite, Tool, Team); Step one, INVITE: first touch conversation inviting them to take a look at a teaser video. Step two, TOOL: having a prospect watch a product and business overview. Step three, TEAM: using third party validation (3-way call or zoom with an upline support team member).

When somebody enrolls on our team, we teach them the ITT system in a simplified two-page launch guide and 15 minute video. We reiterate it on every Zoom call and show our teamies how to use it in order to convert their contacts into customers or distributors. You know your system is effective when someone on your 10th or 100th tier level tells you the two-page guide was easy to follow and they know the three steps they need to follow to succeed. In other words, invest time and effort to set up your team for success!

Rob's Notes: I`ve had the opportunity to speak with Rachel at several large mastermind events where she was a featured speaker. Too many network marketers do not create systems, or they are using outdated systems that they don`t personally revise. For the most part, it`s important to have recruiting, duplication, and retention strategies in your systems. Every great company has one. If you are brand new and don`t have or know how to create one here, is some advice: follow the three-step module Rachel gave. They are simple and powerful!

Audit, Adjust and Apply

Auditing is a technique I discuss with my team while coaching clients. We think about audits with taxation and how it relates to the government, but we need to audit ourselves on a regular basis.

My bank accounts, relationships, calendar and even my health are all audited. If I feel like I`m in a funk, I`ll go back and see what caused me to feel that way and what changed. How did I lose my mojo? Am I not getting enough sleep? How often am I working out? Have I spent personal time in prayer and reading? After answering these questions to find directional solutions, I get myself back on track.

Let`s take it even deeper. This industry is about personal development wrapped around a compensation plan. When was the last time you audited your leadership, your skills and your mindset? If personal development is so crucial in network marketing, how much of your time is focused on it? For some, we are so broken that if we only have ten hours a week to build our business, I recommend spending seven of them on personal growth and the rest on making calls. Why? Because the seven hours will make your three hours of prospecting increasingly more efficient and productive.

Today, many network marketers are reading books, listening to audibles, and podcasts, but don`t apply what they listen to. They don`t go into depth with the "dark and lonely" work of soul searching. It can definitely be terrifying to raise your self-awareness. Imagine coming to grips with the fact that you have a piss poor attitude while unaware of negative self-talk. Practicing self-awareness is key to success.

You think you`re good with people? Great. How many friends do you have? You think you`re a good leader? Awesome. Who`s following you?

In the last eight years I became a millionaire. One reason I was able to achieve this milestone is putting in the work toward my personal development. Back when I started, I was not always strong or as positive as I am today. When I started network marketing, I hated people. Why? In my past experience some people hurt me greatly. Ouch! Imagine trying to be an influencer, trying to recruit and develop relationships with people that you know you won`t be able to trust. Every person is different, make sure to be careful when recruiting and know what intentions people come forward with.

I had to reprogram a lot of negative beliefs from the way I grew up. Nothing against my parents, they did their best and they are awesome, but I grew up hearing, "money doesn`t grow on trees," "who do you think we are, the Rockefellers?" This included the four insidious money blueprint words I heard which I disliked, "we can`t afford that."

Life is a self-fulfilling prophecy. Whatever you believe to be true will undoubtedly become your reality. This is a great time to audit yourself, make adjustments, and apply better habits to your thought process.

The most challenging part of working on your personal development is getting over dark memories from your past and forgiving those who wronged you. This experience improved my skill set, marketing strategies, and made me a better person. During training, a lot of Network Marketers listen but fail to adjust and apply necessary changes. I always remember the quote from Jim Rohn, "If you work harder on yourself than you do on your business, you will be unusually successful."

If you`re spinning your wheels, feeling stuck, dejected, frustrated or even worse, then you`re wallowing in a pit of self-loathing. "Why can I just figure out this business?" Take a step back, look in your journal, ask yourself some hard questions, and do your best to answer them. Hire a life coach, apply new skills you learn. Teach others and you`ll see your life prosper in pulsating ways you never imagined.

Rob's Notes: If you know everything but do nothing, then you know nothing. Don`t become broke. Know it all! If it has value to you, then audit it. Don`t just take notes from this book, apply them to your everyday life! Make this book your recruiting bible for network marketing.

Author: Brittney Mettke

- Joined network marketing in July of 2017.

- Top 10 recruiter in her company.

- Her team currently has over 16,000 members.

- Produced over 60 million dollars in sales volume in less than three years.

- Became a seven-figure earner in less than two years.

- Speaker, a company trainer, a panelist speaker.

- Featured on the cover of "Direct Sales Diva."

"People don't decide their future. They decide their habits, and their habits decide their future."

- F.M. Alexander

am a recovering drug addict. There is no secret to what I have to do if I want to stay alive and sober. It comes down to being intentional, consistent, and patient.

I was an IV heroin user with seven convictions. During my recovery, I was a married mom working at Red Lobster. I worked really hard to do the best job possible at my job. The hard work paid off, and my boss asked if I would be interested in becoming a manager at the location. I worked even harder because it finally felt like I was making progress. I found out after months of training for that management position that the corporate office decided to reject my advancement for an upper management position due to my background. I was devastated and felt like I would never be able to do anything different in life with my past. Instead of letting that hold me back, I used it to give me motivation to do more. I wanted to be more and needed to get over the image I had of my past.

I started to not let my past define me when I started network marketing. I found there were no background checks required. I could own my own business and make an income for my family.

When you get clean, you chase your recovery like you chase the high you used to get from the drugs. Almost like an adrenaline rush. For network marketing to work, I had to be persistent and understand the experience, failures, and successes that came along with it. I needed to create a follow-up system that would work for anyone.

Every person I talk to is an opportunity. I`m always prepared, and no person is left behind. Everyone has potential and I do not judge. Anyone can make this business work. When people saw what I was able to do in network marketing, it showed them that maybe they could do this, as well. People are attracted to possibilities and opportunities for so many different reasons. It`s our job to make sure that we show them what can be achieved when we hit our goals and become successful in business.  Don`t discount anyone. Give everyone a chance to find success, even the people with a past.

Rob's Notes: You will read so many different stories throughout this book. Some leaders had very difficult journeys. These stories are here to show you what is possible, and to empower you to take action right now! In my book, *The Game of Conquering*, and on my website, www.thegameofconquering.com, I explain the different mindsets you face in network marketing. When you know what mindset you have in your business, it can help to propel you to the next level. Brittney shares her incredible story to show you that you can`t let yourself be your biggest obstacle. Some people think network marketing can only work out if you are a certain type of person, and that type of mindset is what doesn`t work out. Don`t rely on your fall back plans and not go all in on becoming successful in something you really want. Defining yourself by your past is just another excuse not to succeed.

It`s hard enough to make anything worthwhile when you have enough income to support yourself. But it is how you show up when it seems like everything is on the line that matters. Brittney is the real deal. Her consistency is what has made her the top tier levels and known as one of the best recruiters in the company.

Connect with Others Authentically

When I started this business, I only had 200 friends on Facebook. Not that many right? As a mother to young kids, I didn't have the chance to get out and meet new people. I was discouraged, and couldn't figure out how to get more connections online. I felt stuck.

Instead of giving myself all these excuses, I changed my mindset and started to see how being an at-home young mom provided me many more opportunities.

I began joining groups on Facebook, meeting new people, and adding friends. Instead of Facebook being a challenge, it turned into an opportunity. I was joining groups with like-minded people and developing organic relationships with them.

I took time to scroll through people's profiles to see who they were. I saw what was going on in their lives and what they were posting about. For example, one post said, "I have a college education and just had to apply to McDonalds." I saw this as an opportunity to connect and encourage that person.

Find people who you think won't be a lead. Anytime I make a post about my business and get a Facebook like, I follow up with a personal message. "Hey, I saw you liked my post, have you ever thought about doing what I am doing?"

Facebook stories are a great way to stay connected. One of my favorite questions to ask is, "Have you ever thought about joining my team?

Yes or No." I`ve been shocked at the people who clicked "yes". It is an opportunity to reach out.

Be intentional with the way you communicate with people. Find a useful platform and set aside time to scroll through all the possible individuals you can reach out to. Make sure to be authentic and honest. When you become honest and authentic with people, it pays off. People want to connect with someone real. It doesn`t matter if it is hard to share. It allows others to connect and see themselves and their life. At first, I wasn`t someone to look up to and follow. I was someone who was working at Red Lobster, not an influencer. But I realized it was the times I shared about working at Red Lobster, and my past that made me authentic. Make sure you are authentic and communicative. These are the most important aspects that attract people.

> **Rob's Notes:** Brittney has been a huge success by spending the majority of her time doing income producing activities. Most network marketers spend too much time making the plan rather than reaching out to new people!

Stay up to Date with your Company, Culture and Trends in your Industry

I spend time every day thinking about individuals on my team. I think about individual people, what is going on with them, and how to connect with them. I also think about people that would benefit in joining my company. It is key to not only spend time connecting with people but thinking about how to add value to them and their lives.

Events are a great way for people to get excited. I signed up thirteen people after my company's conference. I had some great news from the conference, and I wanted to share with others. I would reach out and say, "I was just at a conference and you were on my mind the whole time." It was absolutely true! I intentionally set time aside to think who could benefit, how I can help that individual, and what might excite them about the business.

Be on top of what is going on in today's current events and your company's own news. It will be something that you can share. This can include product launches, trends, or any sort of announcements. These are ways to connect with your contacts.

People love to hear about exciting news. Make sure you share it! You never know who your next super start recruiter or customer might be. Don't miss out on an opportunity to recruit someone by not sharing news and things happening within your business. One time I missed out on a new launch because I wasn't staying up-to-date with current events that week. The launch was providing 40% discounts for teams to attend the next annual conference in Mexico City. I couldn't believe I missed it and the chance to be one of the first sharing that information. I decided I would never miss out on a launch opportunity again, and I haven't.

Have a Way to Connect Again

Recently I was at a conference for our company. I was getting my hair done at a salon and there were dozens of other people from my company there doing the same thing. For two hours the stylist and I talked about life. We spoke about my company and the opportunities it presented. When I left, she had a couple samples from other people she had helped that day from my company. We connected on social media, and a week later I followed up and asked if she liked her samples and if she had any questions. Surprisingly, she loved the products and was really interested in signing up. She told me she received samples from others, but not one person had followed up with her like I did. Dozens of people were willing to give her samples, but not one person had made an attempt to connect with her afterward. Today this wonderful hair stylist is on my team doing an awesome job.

In the beginning, I thought people would come to me. Ha! That definitely never happened. Be the one to reach out. Anytime I meet someone, I make a note to follow up with them whether on Facebook, through phone number, or sending them an email. For the most part, we collect a person's contact information but don't find an opportunity to connect with them afterward.

Always make sure you follow up afterward! Some other ways to reach out are sending a virtual business card in the form of a text, email or direct message on social media. Message prospects, reach out and ask how they would like to be followed up. Take time to send personal messages and ask if they're interested. Give them an expiration date. It helps them know you're serious and you will be talking to them again.

Track your Contacts

One of the ways I track my contacts is through google forms. It doesn't matter where I am, or who I talk to. I always make sure to track my contacts. It's crucial to know who I sampled, how and when I'll follow up with them.

When I first started, I sent out seventy-two samples but never followed up! Talk about the walk of shame. Don't be that person! Be the type who takes his or her connections seriously.

I have specific guidelines in my follow-up instructions. I know who the person is, where we connected, and what I shared. I evaluate their interest (using a one to ten scale) and when their next follow-up is.

Once I was getting my car fixed and ran into the woman who sold me my car. She asked if I was still running my business, and I said yes. She was interested in what I did when I bought my car, but I never followed up with her. Back then, I didn't have a system in place to track follow-ups.

Every new experience is an opportunity to share and recruit. I always make sure to have brochures and samples on me. I'm so glad I got a chance to see the car saleswoman again. It gave me the chance to share the business, and she signed up. I put her info in my google tracking sheet form and knew when to follow up with her. Don't fool yourself thinking you can improve your business without a tracking system. Find one that works for you and work the system.

After the First Contact, Wait a Week and Reach Out

There are different ways to follow up with clients, but I found that waiting a week is the perfect amount of time to follow up and recruit. Don`t have the expectation people will reach out to you. Give them a specific time frame on when you`ll be contacting them.

Sometimes, people won`t follow up due to fear and rejection. They don`t want to hear the word "no." If we hear "no" today, it doesn`t mean it`s "no" forever. In fact, I had several customers tell me "no" and then sign up a week later. One of my top leaders was a "no" person.

A "no," in my opinion, is a "no... not right now." Even a prompt "no" can always be circled back to. People and circumstances change. When someone says "no," it doesn`t mean it`s a reason to stop following up.

Be committed to following up within a week regardless of what happens to the prospect. They may say "no," or they may block you. The point is, change the way you view a "no" response. I knew some prospects would read my text message and never hear from them again. Change the way you look at "no." It means you`re staying consistent with your recruiting. Stick with your system and keep following up. It`s a numbers game and you will get yeses eventually as long as you keep pushing forward.

Set Up your Follow-Up System

No one is ever left behind. A "no" means "no, not right now." These two thoughts convinced me to set up a follow-up system which led me to be the number one recruiter in my company. Now I have over sixteen thousand people on my team. Don`t be the desperate person trying to convince people to join you. If you have to convince people, you`ll have to convince them the rest of the way.

Get over the fear of rejection. What`s the worst thing that can happen? Don`t let a "no" be the end of the story. I once heard that the follow-up only stops when you read an obituary. Make sure to plant the seeds every now and again.

Recruiting isn`t a one-size-fits-all process. You need to know what the person`s interests are and where they sit in life. Start by being a good listener and asking the right questions.

One question I ask is, "On a scale from one to 10, how interested are you?" When prospects say zero, I usually wait two to three months to do the next follow-up. Life changes a lot in three months. For those that answer two to six, they`re on the fence with joining. For that, I follow up every month. If they`re on a scale from seven to 10, then I follow up every week.

I schedule time to connect. I want to be on the phone, video call, or face to face with them in person. I want them to see how much I care. It`s important to find the system that works for you. Stick to it! Continue to follow up and you`ll be surprised to see who says yes in time. Consistency is key so put them in the system if they are a "yes," "no" or "no, not right now." The point is everyone stays in the system. No one is left behind.

When I joined network marketing, I was on food stamps, Medicaid and was going to food banks in order to feed my kids. I was stuck in a marriage where I couldn't financially support my kids. Now I have a business that I built that takes care of us, and it is incredible. I don't have to go through the past miserable experiences anymore and that really means everything to me. My past has always been a place of shame and regret. Now I'm able to talk about and share my story and see how my past helped me get to where I am today. This has been huge in helping impact others. I know there are people out there that need this business. Don't stand in the way of helping others by not recruiting or letting your fears stop you. Set up the system, create follow-ups and help others live a life they never imagined.

Rob's Notes: Successful people do the basics better. Too many network marketers complicate the entire recruiting process. Brittney is a top recruiter and gave you a simple well outlined blueprint to increase your business volume. No, it won't be easy, and yes, you'll still have many rejections but it's 100% worth it. It's time for you to take action and become the conqueror of your business.

Author: Dino Nedelko

- Entrepreneur.

- Coach.

- Networking professional.

- Real estate investor.

- Built businesses in over 40 countries.

- Has a team of over 98,000 people.

- Team has over 20 million dollars in sales.

"There is no journey that's too long if freedom is the destination"

- Dino Nedelko

saw the vision of this industry from the very first day. I hadn't ever been in the industry, but I just knew that this was what I had been waiting for. It was the "freedom" life. I could go out and prove myself and push myself. I could be better and do way bigger things. I knew that I was capable of doing big things if I just got the right opportunity.

One of my early mentors told me, "whatever you believe you will conceive." From the very beginning, I told myself, "I may not have millions, but I am a millionaire." Every single time an obstacle came my way I had the mindset that I was happy it was there. I was ready to deal with it. Tackle it. I needed to overcome it so I knew what to do the next time it would come. In fact, every obstacle that comes my way I know it's getting me closer to my big dreams.

> **Rob's notes:** This is a simple yet so profound statement by Dino. He said, "I may not have millions, but I am a millionaire." Fake it until you make it is a lie that many try alluding to having made more money than they have. What Dino did was different. Dino ACTED AS IF. Act like the million dollar version of you to become the million dollar version of you. How would you talk, smile, posture if you had made a million dollars. Now some of you may say but making that much isn't even close to my goal. That's ok instead of using the word MILLION insert the best version of me. You must become it in your mind before you can actually become it! My good friend Dino who works as hard as anyone I know did just that.

THE BLITZ

I have spent my career traveling and building a business globally. Building a team of over 90,000 members at 4 different continents in less than 5 years in the industry taught me so much about the power of blitzes. You will learn in this chapter that this is one of the fastest and most powerful ways to spice up your business, your results and it will bring the fire inside your groups.

One of the things my mentor told me is that people like to be surprised. The factor of surprise is the best thing that we can have and give. It can be short and sweet. Think about Black Friday shopping. People go crazy for it because it is something that they don`t know what it will be as a doorbuster, and it is temporary. I love The Blitz strategy because you can get a lot done in a very short period of time.

The blitz by itself is an intense action in a short period of time. It helps people to get over their fears and get out of their comfort zone. When I started I didn`t really know **WHY** I would use blitz. I didn`t know **WHEN** I would need to think about this strategy, or **WHERE** to use it. I didn`t know **WHAT** I was doing and what the benefits for my team performance and my business would be. Lastly, I didn`t know **HOW** to get ready for a blitz. I am going to guide you through a simple formula that I call H4W. Why, When, Where, What and How.

How do we know that our blitz system is planned well? If

1. Everyone knows it
2. Everyone does it
3. It works

So, when we are working with blitzes we have to always ask ourselves these 3 questions for the best results possible. That is why good planning and some foundational pieces on how to do it are crucial.

I learned in the very beginning of my network marketing career, the more you take action, the more it becomes a habit and you become the expert. It`s like everything else in life worth having. You have to be willing to put in the work to accomplish the type of success you want to accomplish.

Your first blitz absolutely won`t go without issues and you will need time and repetition to keep improving it. I want you to know it`s absolutely normal if this happens. Key word in creating a great blitz culture and have a large number of people who are ready to take action is CONSISTENCY. Keep improving, keep doing them and you will get better every single day. When it comes to the blitz strategy it really breaks down to being persistent.

It took about six months to a year of me being persistent at this to have my team see the results. When that happened leaders started to duplicate the process by themselves as well. If you don`t yet have a team then by all means implement this with yourself once a month. You could also get your upline or even sidelines involved. Work with what you have and get creative.

1. WHY

Ask yourself this question before you start planning for blitz...WHY? Why are you doing the blitz? Is it because your business is entering the low season? Maybe the holiday season is approaching? Or summer holidays? Or your company just released a new product/system/ incentive/promotion and you want to take massive action to let everyone know about it? Or you want to level up your team`s customer base? Or you want to focus on bringing in a certain group of distributors? There are plenty of options that can be a reason for you to think and plan about the blitz. The most important is to identify that WHY, this will be your main target to build your blitz strategy around it.

I am telling you if you have the right strategy AND you are prepared for it, you can have the best week/month ever!

For example, in the last 3 years I was always super ready for the month of December. It`s the end of the year, many holidays...for the majority of people it is just hard to concentrate and stay on course with their business. The majority of people will tell you that December`s are one of the slowest months in the industry. I personally never agreed with that.

First of all, December is the time when people spend the most money in the entire year, it just depends where they are going to spend it. That is why you have to have the right strategy and you will have a major success. Second of all, you can have the best month in the entire year in December. Just follow the steps below.

2. WHEN

After we have why, we can focus on a specific period that we want to level up the business. I gave you some examples above so let`s break them down.

There are different things happening within your company. Know the company`s plan. Know when there is a promo and plan how best to utilize and use what your company is already offering. Creating a blitz around the existing promotion is a great idea. Or let`s say you have a monthly qualification period and the majority of team members are working very hard to close the month strong and then in the first few days of the new month things are slow – that`s the perfect time for you to create a day or few days blitz to get them back into action immediately.

You also want to look at the season. Several different companies do different things based on the season. If you are building your business internationally, you will want to know when the population is taking time off. Know the seasons of the business, and the seasons of your team. Sales fluctuate. If your sales go down in the summer, you can do a blitz. The holidays are also a great time to plan for a blitz.

Get ready for summer, detox days, boost your immune system for winter blitzes for those who are promoting health and wellness or go back to school days where people are looking for an extra source of income and perfect opportunity for you to create blitz recruiting strategy, tax days return blitzes for those in financial services etc. You see where I am going. Just be creative, think about many seasons, scenarios and you will always find the right time to do the blitz.

3. WHERE

If your blitz requires clear instructions for certain members who want to do it I would always suggest having some sort of special group for those participating. This is helpful for you and the participants. You can clearly prepare them to take the right action, and they know exactly where to go to get information about the blitz. When people know exactly how to do it, their level of fear is lower too.

If people see others doing it and see and hear others talking about results, it makes them take action even at the time that they wouldn`t do it otherwise. Build community and accountability within the participants. If you are doing a three day recruiting blitz and you have forty of your team members who want to go for it...Divide them into pairs and you will have twenty pairs. Now they will work together with their other business partner, help each other, encourage each other and the overall result will be way bigger.

You can do it online, offline or in combination of both.

ONLINE - You can do a special Facebook group and have people come there where you will guide them and give them all instructions on how to do it. If your company or your team is using any kind of funnel systems, special videos, replicated sites, online apps for exposures, virtual online parties, blitz day of webinars every 2 hours, weekend online presentation customer blitz days etc. These are all ideas where to create your blitz. Use social media, it is very effective to use it for promoting your blitz. There are so many apps to reach people, communicate and promote. When you have the right strategy, the right marketing, you can utilize social media very effectively. Again, this can relate to your team members, or it can relate to people that aren`t on your team yet. Depends on the blitz you have decided to do.

OFFLINE - You can do a special offline blitz. You can have your team come together and have recruiting blitzes and give them a certain amount of time to see how many people they can bring aboard. We have done various one day offline blitzes for invitations to the events where we divided our team members to pairs and have them go to special locations like shopping centers, specific professionals depending on your product or service like doctors, health professionals, chiropractors, teachers, taxi drivers, etc. Again use your ideas. You can also do it based on location. Local, international. If your company is opening or just opened a new country and you want to have a strong presence there, create maybe a week blitz where everyone on the team will use any connections they can think of to reach the most people possible in this country. The target for all of them could be an offline meeting you or the company will do in this new country maybe next week.

4. WHAT

Plan for the "whats" of the blitz. What will the theme of the blitz be? What are you focusing on? Is it to get new customers? Is it to get new distributors? Is it to get your existing team into more action by buying more products and do the sampling blitzes in case you have products that can be used as sampling? Are you promoting a new team system and you need a blitz to create the right culture around it? What is it? I already gave some ideas above during the previous sections as well.

Think about some incentives for those who will go for a blitz. Remember one thing. Always try to reward activities and results. Never just results. Some people won`t reach the target they have but they still tried and took action. They deserve to be rewarded as well.

What will the budget for the blitz be? If you are giving away a product or something you have to know how much that will cost you and what is the outcome you are expecting because of it. One of the biggest things I saw is that people want to be rewarded.

People just want to be recognized. Focus on a large number of people and ask them to do small things. You can do a blitz promotion with your existing team and ask them to place a specific order. If they do they will get the gift or maybe some financial reward or however you decide to do it. Be creative, and don`t forget about recognition. Recognize all who qualified and also those who did activity towards it.

 I saw people going for blitzes and working like crazy just because they knew I would create a flyer and put their name and photo on it and recognize them publicly in front of everyone else. Element of recognition is the key to better blitz results. Instead of trying to get a few people to buy a $2k package, shoot smaller and make it wider.

You are going to be blown away at the results you can get from asking a large group of people to do a small thing. You will be able to help so many more people to get results. At the end of the day, that is how it works. Network marketing is all about getting a large number of people to do small things over a long period of time.

Let me give you an example of one of the biggest blitzes I did within the team. The goal was very simple. To give out 20 units of the products to the first 20 people who will sponsor 5 new customers on the team. It was a customer focused blitz. It was also focused on new customers and not on existing members.

I knew that giving out that much product would cost me almost $2,000 so I took this as foundation to determine the number of customers they would need to achieve in order to qualify for the reward of the blitz. After the entire blitz was planned I was ready to launch. When I launched the blitz, it took less than 8 days and we had all twenty qualifiers. In less than eight days we got one hundred new customers on the team plus a few hundreds more from those who maybe sponsored one or more, but were not fast enough to get into the first twenty who collected the reward.

The effect of that kind of blitz can`t even be measured just a few days after the blitz because this changes your business for the better for years. These customers will keep ordering. But instantly from the eight days blitz, the reward for me was way bigger than $2,000 that it cost me to give away the rewards. Again, I am sharing all these practical examples with you to make your brains start to think in direction of how many different options you can do. As you can tell, I simply love blitzes!

5. HOW

We learned why, when, where and what are we doing in previous chapters. We have these 4 things in place now.

HOW is the most important part. I call it the heart of the blitz. Create a strategy. This is the execution. Because if you do not have a specific action plan in place, if you don`t have clear instructions, you will struggle.

First, take your why, when, where and what so you can decide HOW are you going to implement and launch your blitz. I will guide you through how with another example, I believe seeing examples is the best way to really understand how this works.

EXAMPLE: BLITZ SATURDAY – every 2 hours opportunity meeting from 8 am to 8 pm.

Let me break this example down to the basics and you will quickly figure out HOW this works.

WHY in this case is to boost distributor acquisition in the team with all day business opportunity meetings.

WHERE – this example can be implemented online and offline. I have done both of them multiple times. If it`s offline, then you will have a place or an office where you will have an opportunity meeting starting every 2 hours, if it`s online – the same thing – just online. Let`s say we are doing it online for this particular example.

WHEN – in example we decided to do the weekend because the majority of people are more free with their schedule over the weekend and maybe we do it first weekend of the month if the season and the time is expected to be lower for your company.

WHAT – online business opportunity meetings and we decide to reward everyone who have at least 10 prospects during the day at the meeting with special public recognition in front of the team and for everyone who will achieve the goal they will also get a special one hour training with you or any other top leader in the company or in the industry. That way we make it attractive and many people will go for it and of course the biggest impact they will see is their business is going to have a major growth.

HOW – this is now the most important piece. Creating a complete strategy from beginning to the end. In order to create this blitz a huge success we will need to look into strategies and create steps like:

1. Create inviting strategy – all members who will be ready to go for it, will be able to simply copy it and reach out to as many potential prospects as possible to invite them for blitz Saturday

2. We will create special group (it can be facebook group, chat, whatsapp, whatever you and your team use) where team members will be given special instructions when to start inviting, how to invite, how to track activities etc)

3. Since we are doing an online blitz we can also use options like Facebook Watch Party to stream every meeting to thousands and thousands of potential prospects in our members network

4. Reward and recognition strategy - what is in for them, those who are going to go for a blitz. What is the potential result they will get in their business if they go all out and do it.

5. If we want to make the most out of it we also have to create post blitz follow up strategy

These are just a few of the ideas on how we can absolutely rock blitzes. The planning isn`t just the activity of doing the blitz. The planning also includes everything leading up to it and also after the blitz. You have to schedule the pre and post work of a blitz or you miss out on the whole reason for doing it. You have to give them the vision and they have to understand why they want to be part of it. If they don`t understand, they won`t plugin. And as we said at the beginning, the element of surprise is the greatest form of engagement.

Implement it inside the blitz either with special reward, gift, or anything like that.

Network marketing is at an exciting time. People keep mastering the industry, but there is still a huge place for us to improve and take it to the next level. Blitzes can play a huge part of your business and your success. Study them very well and master it. You will never regret it. I am proud of you already for just coming that far and being ready to learn all these amazing chapters in this book. Keep learning but most importantly keep taking action. Don`t be afraid of mistakes and failures that will come as a consequence of taking action. This is the normal process of growth. I believe in you and wish you all the best. Cheers to your success!

Rob's notes: I have seen first hand Dino take this blitz strategy and fine tune it to have incredible results. If you are new don`t get overwhelmed as you can keep coming back to this layout and make it your own over time. If you already have an existing team I highly suggest you implement this Blitz strategy asap. You need focus and your teams especially need focus. Regular blitzs will increase sales in your business.

Author: Tyrica Hendricks Duckett

- Wife, mother, caregiver.

- Entrepreneur, philanthropist.

- Started network marketing in 2015.

- Became top 1% of the company in 2 years.

- Bachelor`s in political science 1995, Master`s in Administrative Management in 2000.

- Became six figure earner in 2018.

- 99 members in her frontline.

- Downline of 56,000 and growing daily.

- Estimated retail earnings of eight million dollars monthly.

- Member of Delta Sigma Theta Sorority Incorporated Inc.

"May your choices reflect your hopes, not your fears."

-Nelson Mandela

It`s not always what you know, but sometimes it is who you know. My mom taught me this at a very young age, and it has helped me grow into a successful businesswoman, a philanthropist, and an outstanding member of my community. While I was growing up, my mom took me to social events. I would often be the only little girl there! She took me to both political movements and social balls. I mean, you name it, I was there. In our community, people used to see me as "that little girl that went to those events." At an early age, I was taught to network and socialize with all types of people from diverse ethnic backgrounds.

Create a culture that you can network in. Who you know and how you treat people matters. I`ve always been in situations where I would be friends to the ones that didn`t have any. It`s my nature to be nice to everyone, especially those who need support. This is why I`m capable of networking with so many different people. The culture I was raised in involved being social and understanding diversity within communities. These are huge qualities to possess in this industry.

How do you feel about your circle of friends? What about your community? I love my community. I love being able to make connections everywhere I go and interact with different individuals. I`ve been blessed by the relationships I created. One thing that helped me do this is really knowing my niche.

When talking about your niche, I`m talking about really looking at your life from a bigger perspective, seeing who you`re connected to, and what interests you share with others. You have to be able to use what you have, and everyone has different niches. You may live in the same neighborhood as somebody else, but that doesn`t mean you possess the same interests. The only aspect you have in common is living in the same area. Other examples of niches include being in a sorority, on a sports team or a hobby you like, such as cooking or swimming. It really doesn't matter what it is. One niche for me is being passionate about the community I grew up in.

When I got my business running, I shared my products with all my niches. I began to use them in my network. For example, one of my niches is staying involved with my sorority over the years. I sent out individual text messages to my "sisters" letting them know I'm always looking for revenue streams while discussing my business. I let them know they could buy the product, join my team, or do both. Be willing to talk to everyone, but don't judge and make choices to determine if someone is a good fit or not for the company. The same day I got a text back from one of my sorority sisters asking if she could really make money. I let her know, "Yes, you can!" Two days later, she joined my team and now we're both top producing earners. This goes back to what my mother taught me: it's not always what you know but who you know that matters. I was raised in a community where we were taught to stay connected and to care about each other because we all matter.

Going back to my college days, when I returned home, I signed up for the Big Brother and Big Sister Program. My parents always said, "to whom much is given, much is expected." I was taught to give back. When I was assigned a little sister, I found out her grandmother died, and she was facing major family problems. I became her foster parent and eventually her legal guardian. We are 11 years apart in age. When I went through the adoption process, I had an amazing support system of family and friends that made the adoption process easy to complete. It was who I knew that supported me to be a successful single mom by choice at a young age.

I teach my team that your life experiences will allow you to see what networks are strictly unique for you. It could be a church community, a soccer team, or a salsa club. For example, if your daughter is in girl scouts, talk to the leader and get to know their community. Now my daughter is way past that age group and that niche network isn`t open to me anymore.

The idea is to find your niches. Figure out the things in life that are unique and support you. Find what you like and spend time with it. Whatever you decide, make a commitment to be the best at it. It doesn`t matter if you are an individual in network marketing or any kind of business, just do what you love doing and be the best at it!

Rob's Notes: Clichés are timeless principles. You will hear this cliché over and over again. Stop prejudging others. Tyrica said it. Be willing to talk to everyone. Some of my best contacts failed in network marketing because they didn`t give it their best shot while others absolutely crushed it making millions of dollars. By following Tyrica`s strategy, you learn much about this business. I wish I had known Tyrica before meeting her at one of my recent masterminds. She could have shaved years off my first book. It took me seven years to write the book *The Game of Networking*. The entire book focuses on how to network, and notice I didn`t say network marketing. Network first! Be a good friend first!

Here is a direct quote from *The Game of Networking*, "Your best protection strategy is forever your network. Ability alone won`t spare you. Not even education, nor the government, will spare you. A network is your best protection and is your best insurance policy. Be the best you. You can`t be Steve Jobs! Richard Branson would have been horrible had he tried to be Steve Jobs. Steve Jobs would have been awful had he tried to be Richard Branson. They both have had an insane amount of success, but both of them did so because they focused on becoming a better version of themselves. Networking is not only your insurance policy, it is the key to happiness. Networking is the foundation of life."

The Brand of You

From day one, brand yourself. Think about what you`re known for and what makes you unique. Think about why people would buy from you or join your team over anybody else. I made sure everyone knew I was doing network marketing. Whatever their opinion was about it, was just that, their opinion. I listed how people could help me. They could buy products, join, or refer someone to my team, or recommend people to shop on my website. As a philanthropist and someone that is continually giving back, I branded myself as someone that can help others. I began to be recognized for what I was doing. I intentionally branded myself as "sassy and classy." Others would say I`m always classy or proper. I made a post about this on social media today.

Someone once told me, "Your brand should tell people who you are, what you are, and how you do it. Be yourself, brand you." Create a culture around your brand even if it`s something new. Stay true to yourself while growing as a person in this business. Be true to your values and open to constantly learning. Understand that sometimes the middle is going to look different than what the end will look like. Stay focused on your goals, and don`t dwell on the process.

One thing I learned is when you master enrollment, you master life. You are enrolling every day. When you go home and try to get your kids to eat dinner, you may not realize you`re enrolling them in the idea of getting them ready for dinner time. In sooth, the skills you learn in network marketing not only apply in business, they apply in everyday life. I have worked on having skills to network. They are great skills to have, but it takes more than networking skills to be a professional network marketer. Be willing to always be working on skills that can uplevel your business.

Do what you say you will. Show up as the same person on social media. I`m always the same person from start to finish. I am always myself whether you get to know me from a business perspective or around town. It is important to always be yourself. It`s important to live your brand.

I never change once someone is on my team, I am the same person always. People may not always love the real me, but they can be sure that I`m not going to turn my back on them. I`m the exact same person from start to finish. I can only be me. It`s my superpower!

People that know me now know I`m the same person they met when we met for the first time. Brand yourself so people know who the real you is. Like it, love it or hate it, the choice is yours. My mom always taught me people may not like what you say, but if it`s the truth, then they`ll always respect you later. If you believe enough to do it, then you don`t need approval from anyone else. Sometimes people lack confidence and look to others for approval. It`s significant that you do things for you.

Time and time again, some people aren`t confident enough to share their story. From what I`ve learned in engaging with so many adults, there are many men and women out there who lack self-confidence. I now teach my team how to be self-confident. Learning this attitude change requires a simple fix while working on their self-development. Once, a team member told me the reason she joined was to only grow her confidence. She really didn`t need money. Now she looks and feels more confident than ever before and that means everything to her! I love how confidence changes people for the better like it did with her.

Occasionally, people are afraid to open their mouths. They`re scared to say what they want. They`re just scared to do it! One time, I was talking to a woman on my team who said she bumps into the same woman on the bus several times a week. When she sees her, the woman compliments her products. Instead of using this opportunity as a way to share the product, she only says thank you. The point is she lacks confidence in sharing her products every time she`s around the same lady. For me, confidence was installed at an early age, and now I carry it throughout my life. As an adult, I realized not many people are taught this skill. Confidence and self-esteem play a huge role for me as a leader. Teach confidence!

I`m proud of my business and love what I do. Be willing to tell everyone about your business! Say it the way you say it, let it come naturally. Always be the person and the brand. Never devalue your business and don`t let anyone else either. Tap into your network. Literally tell everyone you know what you are doing! Be that person they know as a professional network marketer. No matter what it is, you have to make people respect you. If you are ashamed of your own business, people will not join you.

On occasion, I`m at red carpet industry events with my husband and encounter many celebrity wives and female companions who`ll come up to me and ask about my products. When I tell them what I do, they get excited about the business! These are some of my biggest clients. The point is, you never know who you`re going to meet that will change your life. Even though this business is not for everyone, don`t be the person who decides who it`s for. It`s each person`s choice to make.

Do you believe in what you say, do you believe in yourself? People respect honesty. Don`t lie and don`t make up a story. You should tell your story and speak your truth. They may not like you or what you say, but they`ll respect you if you`re honest. Believe what you say and say it with confidence. When you do this, you`ll naturally incorporate this value into your product presentation.

Rob's Notes: Spot on Tyrica! I asked one of the most successful people I know this very simple question, what is your top tip for happiness and success? He summed it up with one of the simplest yet brilliant answers. "Rob, do what you say you`re going to do when you say you`ll do it. If you do this one thing, you`ll build trust and self-esteem. You`ll build credibility with others, and it`ll change everything." You are your brand. You may love your company and your team, but you can`t control what happens to them. Remember everything you put your effort into. Everything you do is part of your brand. The process begins and only continues with you becoming the person you want to recruit.

Give Back to your Niches

On my 45th birthday, I launched a nonprofit organization. I called it the "Tyrica and Robert Duckett Hope Foundation." Ever since I was a kid, it`s always been my dream to have a nonprofit foundation. Hope stands for "Helping Other People Every day." Without a consistent network, the foundation wouldn`t exist. I`m always looking to give back to my communities. When I started network marketing, I was working full time and saw this as a chance to fund my philanthropic work.

My business launched in July of 2015 and in March of 2016 I was laid off from my job. I thought this was God pushing me. I had no intention of leaving my job, but I got laid off. Although my company slowly laid people off, I never thought of doing network marketing full time. I thought if I got laid off, I would just find another full-time job. You see I didn`t know when I would get laid off, but when I did, I was the happiest laid-off person ever.

It doesn`t take money to make money. It takes creativity. Layoffs and trials become huge advantages as they force you to find new ways to be creative. Such challenges are time trials. It was the value of creativity that guided me to look at all my options and really see network marketing as something I could do. I knew I was highly employable but had a lot of family things going on. This was a great time to make the change over to network marketing.

God let me know clearly, I had other things to focus on. I give credit to God for setting me up for greatness. I understood how much money I needed to make to replace my previous income and went to work to make it happen. I set myself a timeline of a year to succeed, and if

I didn`t, I could get another job. My motivation was higher than ever to succeed so I could give back to the people and community that had supported me.

The products aligned perfectly with my vision of giving back to my circle of friends and donating to communities that I supported. It was a marvelous feeling. The product was perfect and made sense for my consumer base. The products sold themselves. You either give your clients a vision to see it or you don`t. Simple as that.

With my new business, I`ve been able to travel around the world helping women and girls in dozens of countries. I`ve always been a person who wanted to give back and strengthen other communities. Network marketing made that possible for me and in my niche community. I looked at this opportunity as a means to do my philanthropy work and honestly didn`t imagine how it would turn out. I never thought in my wildest dreams I would be a top team leader with salespeople on my team and recognized by the company. I only knew I had a product that would sell itself. I never thought this industry would be able to give back to the community I love, but it did.

Niches are Really your Riches

My niche is my network! One of my useful business skills is sending out text messages and emails to those looking for additional revenue streams explaining about my business. I let prospects know what I`m selling, invite them to learn more about my team, or ask for a referral. Some may be interested and others not, but I appreciate any of these three options. Make sure you are showing people how they can help you. Be direct with them.

When my affiliates don`t think they know enough people, but in reality they know someone. I tell them to start exploring. I have them think about experiences that are unique to them. If they think they don`t know many people, then it`s time to get out and start networking. You always have to give insight to your team and make suggestions. As soon as that stops, your recruiting will decrease. When I stopped traveling for work, my contact list went down. At that point, I had to find a way to purposefully get myself out of the house so I could start making direct conversation with people again.

This also happened with one of my affiliates. She`s a stay-at-home mom who had a son that played sports. One day she decided to introduce this opportunity into her son`s sports community. She was able to do this because of her involvement with the other sports parents. This was a unique experience, and the timing was right. She knew her son wouldn`t be in high school sports forever, but those parents could be customers forever. She realized networking with those parents could produce life changing opportunities while maintaining good relationships with them.

I always tell people, "Let me know if you know anyone who would like to make extra money." It could be them or someone at church they know. I kill two birds with one stone or turn one client into two.

I love the events and the personal interactions that come with hosting parties. You meet all kinds of amazing people at a party. It's a great way to expand your circle. Think of parties like putting gold nuggets in your basket. This is what networking is all about, to expand your own circle of influence and get to know others you never met. For some it's uncomfortable sitting next to someone at a table you don't know. Do your best to step out of your comfort zone to be more in tune with what you are capable of offering to others. That's your friendship first, business second and product third. Your fruit and butter are always your family and friends, but new connections also present more opportunities.

Most of my team members aren't necessarily people I knew. Some of them were referrals. Some of my very first members were referred to me by a guy I went to elementary school with. One day I texted and asked him if he knew a couple of women that wanted to make extra money right now. He referred me to several women who are now on my team. It was totally unexpected and surprising. Most people wouldn't think to reach out to someone from several decades ago. Dig out your connections; people are there! Another time, I reached out to my prom date from high school. I told him he could buy these amazing products for his daughter, and he did. Open your eyes and go outside of the obvious. You will miss out on an entire network by passing over people you don't see as your "typical" customer or support.

At my first big vendor event, over fifty thousand people attended. I set a goal of how many new business connections I wanted to make. Don't put a goal on the product; make the connections first and work with them! At that event I signed up five people which turned into hundreds of affiliates joining their teams all underneath me. I was also able to get hundreds of emails to add to my email list.

Not too long ago I remember one of my team members told me how she used to go watch her son`s basketball practices during the winter sports season. As she watched her son from the stands, she would take her product samples with her to organize. Next thing you know, you see parents start coming over asking her what she had. She began selling her products at her son`s practices. She was willing to do something quite unconventional back then. She stepped out of her comfort zone and it worked. Even though her son is no longer playing sports, she applied this same marketing tactic anywhere she went that had large crowds of people. Creativity works when you step outside the box to bring unexpected clients.

This business works for anyone who has time to invest and wants a supportive team along with it. This includes people with full time jobs. I teach people how to incorporate this business into their lives.

The support I get comes in all forms and sometimes not directly from my team. For example, some of my biggest supporters never bought my products but only sent me referrals. These supporters talk about my business with their circle of friends. Again, you never know where your results will come from. Everybody on my team knows about the power of referrals.

One of my foundation`s initiatives that I take pride in is a program for girls in Kenya called "Girl Power." These girls meet twice a month to talk about confidence and their vision for the future.

When the program started, our instructors asked the girls what they wanted to be. They said house cleaners and clerks. I`ve seen what`s possible with this program. The girls make vision boards and it`s wonderful to interact with their mothers from various walks of life. Their culture is incredible.

As the program grew, so did the girls. Now they say they want to become doctors, lawyers, teachers, and journalists. This program exists due to funding from my network marketing business. To tell you the truth, starting this foundation has brought me heavy influence with others around the world. God gives you more than you ask for if you allow God to point you in the right direction. Do your best to use your niche in helping others to see their goals and dreams.

Rob's Notes: If you network properly you will learn to generate endless leads from referrals! Tyrica is an ample example of a leader who always implements valuable support to her network.

Author: Eva Bergstrom

- Entrepreneur, business advisor, and an avid traveler.

- Seven years of experience in network marketing.

- Eva gives brilliant insight into the fundamental skills.

- 1978, winner of Finnish National Hairdressing Competition

- 1979 placed 10th overall in the Athens European National Hairdressing Championship.

- 2nd in the Australian National Hairdressing Championship in 1981.

- Won the Australia Society of Makeup Artistry and award for Excellence in 2004.

- From 1995 to 1998, she studied Medical Herbalism.

- In 2014, she won the award for Leadership.

- She won the award for Wealth Creator in 2015 and the Power Ranking Award in 2018.

- Part of the Millionaires Club in 2016.

- Partner Council in 2018, 2019 and 2020.

"World needs Truthfulness,
Compassion, Forbearance."

I remember the exact moment asking myself a question that would change the course of my life. During that time, I was 57 years old working as a freelance makeup artist. For 12 years, I worked countless hours in featured films, photoshoots, and commercials. When I woke up, I worked long hours on my feet only to come home exhausted and repeat the whole process the next day. One day I truly asked myself, "Is this all there is to life?" This couldn`t be what life was supposed to be about. Having a freelance business wasn`t as glamorous as I thought. As a freelancer you always want to be first on the employers` minds so they give you more business and referrals.

Keep in mind, all payment ceases for a freelancer if you`re not working. One year, there were massive floods in Brisbane. You really couldn`t drive anywhere due to the amount of water. I was six months without work, and it was a really difficult challenging part of my life. Clearly, I didn`t have any work coming in and was desperately trying to find my next job. I did the math and realized I would have to work until I was 80 years old to keep supporting myself. My body gave me signs that working 12-hour days on my feet wasn`t sustainable for my health as I got older! The fact is every person has a story on why they made the change to network marketing.

Rob's Notes: I`ve traveled all the way to Australia to speak to Eva`s teams. I`ve heard her incredible story many times. We heard about other co-authors and the tragedies they endured. These are the ones to recognize if they have success. For the most part, we prejudge way too often in network marketing. We think, "I can`t approach them because they aren`t successful enough," and sometimes the opposite, "I can`t approach them because they are way too successful." Eva is a perfect example of a leader who had success but was looking for more! Don`t be afraid to approach your chicken list. If you know highly successful people, talk to them. All winners share the same circle with successful people.

Reach out to them. They're the ones that understand business, leverage, and have more influence. As Wayne Gretsky said, "you never make any of the shots you don't take." Pay close attention to several following tips from Eva.

Eva wants us to be aware of our story and of our client's stories too. Find out what makes your prospects interested in network marketing. Is it a personal struggle, a goal, the opportunity, or is it the product?

Prior to working as a freelance makeup artist, I owned and operated a hair salon. I started in the business when I was 17 years old and made a name for myself in the industry and across other make up competitions. By 21, I was the youngest person to rank number one in the country and quickly rose to the top in Europe. When I relocated to Australia, I took top rank. Learning how to adapt to new environments in these competitions was key for me to step out of my comfort zone. The momentum shift in my business was happening, and I was excited for what was about to come.

What is your prospect's previous experience in business? What experiences have they had in their personal lives and business that made them want to join network marketing? When I relocated to Australia, I spent eight months learning English before I bought my own salon. Keep in mind the average business lasts three years before changing hands or closing down. My salon was open for nineteen years in Central Sydney. It felt like my home, and my clients were my honored guests. I loved being able to host and entertain everyone. I was one of the first salons ever in the country to offer champagne, liquor, and coffee to clients. The business taught me where to look for the best quality traffic flow to attract more clients. For example, being next to a coffee shop and food establishment meant more foot traffic to my salon, which meant more clients.

I also owned a brick and mortar business which was difficult to run. At times, I came across maintenance issues which were challenging to manage. This required switching from location to location. When I gave my store front a much-needed upgrade, the expenses skyrocketed, and the cash flow didn`t increase as I anticipated. To add on, overhead and managing staff created more problems. I would spend countless hours training my staff, who would then leave while taking clients with them. The staff turnover was a miserable experience to deal with.

Despite the struggles, I pushed on and worked hard at my salon. Then one day my whole world crashed like a dinner plate. I lost my fiancé three days before our wedding day and with that everything else. Everything fell apart. I had worked for decades on my dream and suddenly everything disappeared. This period was one of the hardest obstacles I dealt with in my life. In the end, I shut down the salon, relocated to Brisbane, and started my freelance makeup gig.

Ask yourself these questions. Why did I start network marketing? What events led me to this industry? As mentioned, my salon business was very costly and at times hard to operate. I was constantly worrying about my clients, my staff, and their clients. At first, freelancing felt fantastic. Again, there was no huge overhead, building or staff, but the atmosphere felt anxiety-ridden and fearful. I was always chasing the next job and never felt very secure. One day I asked myself, "Is this all there is to life?" Even though I had a couple businesses up and running, a network marketing opportunity didn`t present itself until I came across a product.

At the time I was looking for an anti-aging product. The product I found gave me phenomenal results and the opportunity to join a network marketing company. Although I had some resistance to this industry, my gut feeling told me this would be a life changer. I slowly started learning more about network marketing. I already had so much experience with traditional business and freelance, I wondered how this would be a great fit for me. Even though with the passing of my fiancé, losing my salon, and starting a make-up gig, it makes me anxious to think how I could make more money entering a type of business realm.

Most businesses have prospects, what questions do they have, what fears do they have about the business, what do they feel is lacking in their lives? What are they searching for? I understand why people have a negative approach to network marketing. I used to be the same! But now, I see how often people lose out on the opportunity because they fear the unknown and put their barriers up. Sometimes I wonder how much I've lost in the past when I put my barriers up. Now I think, "this is the only way." I started this business when I was 57 years old and remember when I made my first $25 check. My reaction was, "Yes! I made money!" My heart was content because the sale closed, and I didn't worry about how much it was. Now it was time to keep repeating those sales for more success. To give you a better idea, network marketing is tangible. The numbers are there. It is a real business that has value. The traditional business model has evolved. This is a new business unlike I've ever experienced. Businesses can't succeed using the old ways. Compare the first flip phone with the iPhone X. Network marketing is the new smart way available today in doing business.

In the beginning, the hardest challenge I anticipated was the criticism people would give me about the "new business" I was doing. For me, it was quite embarrassing at first. I built up a good number of followers, and then I was going to tell them about this? Who even knew what network marketing was? At first it almost felt like a bag of shame, but I couldn't let that get to me. Not with something this new and promising. The best part I discovered was if I was sick or on holiday, I could still work the business. It keeps working even if I have to take a break from it. I get an income when leaving for the holidays. To be honest, I`m still blown away by that. After all the experience in owning businesses and working in freelance, I could have never imagined this would be possible.

So, what opportunities are you offering to your prospect? It`s important to know what you`re offering. I couldn`t let the opinion of others phase me or the business. I became passionate about my business and what our company offers. I`m a proud introvert and didn`t know how I would come across when socializing with others. After the first try, I connected with many amazing people at my first meeting and felt part of a supportive community.

In addition, being single also helped to develop meaningful relationships. My status opened the door to let me see what kind of independent financial freedom was out there through network marketing. There are opportunities everywhere. Know your prospects well enough to know what similar opportunities they have compared to you. Open the door for them and be their mentor.

Rob's Notes: I have so many takeaways from Eva`s insights. One big takeaway is our questions sometimes are the answers. For example, she mentions several different questions in her five main headline points. She understands the best network marketers out there are really good at asking the right questions. Think of what type of recruiting questions might expand your business. The more you ask you, the more you`ll learn and make the right proper choices.

Author: Alyssa Cowart

- Master distributor.

- Eight years in network marketing.

- When she got in the business, she was a single mom with two young boys.

- First two years she became a six-figure earner.

- Three-years later became a seven-figure earner.

- Public speaker, trainer, podcaster.

- In her spare time Alyssa likes to travel and inspire others to dream big with implemented planned actions.

"Winners are not people that never fail, but people that never quit."

sn`t it annoying when you hear anyone can do this business, like driving a car? You think, sure they had success, but how does that relate to me? I`ll go into depth about some of my struggles and how they led me to create a step by step blueprint that took my business to another level. It is also what has helped me help others have success in this business.

When I was 15 years old and in the 10th grade, I had my first son. When I received my high school diploma, he was two years old. During the day, he would be in daycare, and I would go to high school. After school, I would do homework. Then I would go to work waiting tables at night. The feeling of being broke is hardening.

I found equal opportunity in network marketing. It was something I didn`t experience with waiting tables. It doesn`t matter what age, race or education you have. Anyone can do this business as long as they have the passion, drive, and dedication to succeed.

I went from a struggling mom with two kids, waiting tables and cleaning buildings at night to making substantial money. I`m passionate about sharing my experiences. This is a true story of why I fell in love with this new industry. For eight years and counting, I have been able to change many people`s lives in my company. There were incredible life-changing results I`ve seen in health, wellness and financial freedom obtained by the members of my team. When you invest in people, it changes your life. Through building strong relationships online and offline, you can really make an impact on someone`s business network.

In the Business of Relationships

Discover the number one reason why most network marketers don`t have high retention. Get to know people and invest time in them. Distributors are so caught up in their numbers that they forget about the relationships. When they do this, prospects are gone the next month because you haven`t built the relationship. What does a person need, what is their love language and how can I support them? I have so many different personalities on my team, and there are many ways to lead, support, and uplift your teams` spirits. Some of them want to do their own thing. Others need lots of love and cheering. In most cases with retention, the problem is not the product but the type of relationships that developed. The fact is, if you have a relationship with your customers, then they`re more comfortable talking to you about anything. When your customers know that you really care about them, they open up. If that line of communication isn`t open, then we can lose our affiliates and customers.

Understand your audience and who your clients are. I ask my team who their target market is and if they say everyone, I tell them they`re wrong. The reality is, they`re not going to connect and have a personal relationship with everyone. Know who your ideal clients are going to be and know how you`re going to keep them engaged. For example, I`m not going to recruit someone who is collecting model airplanes, even though I like model airplanes. We may not have a real connected relationship. Make sure you know who your exact recruit is.

Rob's Notes: Alyssa is spot on! Culture is the number one most important piece to retention. In my twelve years of experience, I`ve seen most distributors leave their companies due to the lack of appreciation they have with their customers. Customers will typically stop ordering when they don`t hear back from you from time to time. John Maxwell says it best, "People don`t care how much you know until they know how much you care." Culture is your best retention, and we`ll discuss this more.

You are what you recognize. In other words, if your team doesn`t see a business module providing value, then it won`t matter to them! Figure out what the most important aspects to your culture are.

Here are a few examples of recognition. Have a good social media group for your team, where other members can post in addition to their profiles to attract new customers. Create some ways to recognize your new potential distributor with a curiosity post. "Welcome our next new member to the team." Show customer engagement with an appreciation system of examples such as thank you cards, regular follow up texts/voice messages, or anything that makes your customer feel valued. If your company doesn`t have a rank to recognize members when they make their money back, then create recognition to add that team value.

But Rob, I don`t have a team yet! That`s ok, because if you`re reading this book you`re committed. As Stephen Covey says, "Begin with the end in mind!" In other words, we`re preparing you for the right mindset to become a leader so you can have a large team. I`ve spent time working with Alyssa at my masterminds and she`s as genuine as she sounds in her book. Pay attention to her lessons. Now let`s learn about the importance of building your business online with Alyssa!

Online Connection

Too many network marketers are doing it all wrong! Recruiting is about follow-up and making meaningful connections, not copying and pasting the same posts on social media. You should always present different qualities. The worst struggle is when I see someone doing everything right, but I see them not making progress. What may work for me won`t work for everyone. Distributors need to understand their voice and verbiage. Stop constantly looking for the one golden ticket to success. It doesn`t work that way. People can`t just copy and paste any more. It`s important to get the product information out there but share it in a unique way as if you`re speaking to your customer. Think about how different you would talk to a mom with five kids who is working full time versus a twenty-year-old college kid who is hustling trying to figure out what to do with his life. Know what content will strike more to your diverse audience.

Today, there are so many of us doing network marketing. So, what sets you apart from everyone else? The thing that makes marketers different is the relationship. People are coming to you because of your relationship with them. They can get their information from so many places but come to you because you`re unique. They click with you. Sometimes, we unintentionally recruit prospects we share nothing in common with. It`s essential to write who you`re looking for and how you`re going to have a relationship with them. Make sure you`re being authentic to your social media audience. Your personal feed doesn`t need to look like a big commercial. Be personal, people want to connect with you and not just an ad. Share real-life situations and be real. Be transparent with yourself while sharing your product.

With the exception of Sunday, our team has a power hour every day of the week. Once you achieve a certain rank you can host a power hour. We all take turns. Power hours take place on zoom video meetings, which are hosted by the leader in the company. We use this time to build our work relationships. There are exact tasks to do while others do training. We really do this company-wide and anyone is welcome. It`s a time to focus on the business and get things accomplished. It`s been amazing to see the connections and relationships that strengthen during our power hour meetings. Be creative when you are finding a way to connect online. The power hour is what connects us to prospects and customers outside the industry.

In today`s digital age, it`s common to see sponsors being added to 40 different Facebook groups, three different text threads or six different zoom calls within the first week. This is good exposure for our sponsors but sometimes may be overwhelming. Could you imagine starting a corporate job on your first day and your new boss put all the files, policy papers, and everything you needed on your desk and said, "Here is everything, good luck!" That would be crazy. Today, we don`t take the time to get to know our clients or lay out the basic foundations for them. When affiliates join on the first day, they think they need to know everything about the company and its compensation plan. Training takes time. It`s vital to have digital information available for your affiliates if they need to obtain more information. They don`t need to know everything right away when they start. It`s too overwhelming.

Building Authentic Relationships

There are so many people on my team I never hear from. The only time I`ll see or hear from them is at the annual Christmas party. It`s paramount to know who your clients are, what they like, and what they`re interested in. Some of your clients may love to connect only once or twice a year. Keep them in touch with the community and form a location where your members can conduct meetings, such as at an office space. Get to know them. Find out what is going on in their lives; they will become your friends. People like to connect authentically in many different ways. If you love events like I do, then your customers may like them too. Be willing to throw the party of the year in order to build those connections.

If your customers or team members love to connect directly face to face, make sure you`re setting up events with good entertainment. One good example is having a retreat. Our company has leadership retreats for those who want to bond more with their team. One day, I told one of my good friends, "I need you to get on an airplane and not ask questions, let me know when you land, the final destination is a surprise!" She did it. She got on the plane and came to see what I had to say about network marketing at one of my retreats. It was an incredible experience for her. She loved the music, the light shows, and the public speakers. Everything stood out to her. She not only joined but signed up members from her book club, as well.

Be careful listening to other people`s opinions. Sometimes it`s gossip! People make opinions about you without even knowing you. They hear stories and grab onto them. I was able to form many good friendships since I stopped listening to other people`s opinions and focused on authenticity. Being authentic is huge! We get so caught up on outward appearances. You have to stay authentic to yourself and who you are inside. In other case scenarios, people have different opinions about what authenticity is. You can`t define authenticity for other people. It looks different for everyone. Know what authenticity looks like for you. At times, I`ve been discredited for my looks or even for the handbag I was holding. Don`t judge how a person looks and make time to find authenticity in everyone.

Rob's Notes: The bigger an online presence becomes for one`s business, the greater the demand is for an offline presence! Think about it like this. Is there a difference between going to a concert and listening to music in your car or what about going to a live sporting event versus watching it on live tv? Yes of course there is. Leaders are born at events. Authentic relationships are truly made in person. Use online platforms to build speedy connections with people and offline communication to solidify those fresh authentic relationships.

You Aren't for Everyone and that's Ok

Let`s accept it, we are scared of rejection, people don`t like to hear the word "no." Accept the fact that God gave us different personalities for a reason. Not everyone is going to like who you are. I would love everyone to like me, but it isn`t humanly possible. God didn`t design us that way. We don`t physically have time to have super close relationships with everyone. Don`t feel the need to have everyone like you because you know you are capable of creating meaningful friendships with the ones that matter. Don`t be afraid to reach out and connect. Let`s talk about one situation that exemplifies my point. The waitress comes around and asks about coffee. I say no thank you, and she doesn`t take it personally. When I leave, she gives me my bill and asks if I want coffee. Surprisingly, I needed the energy and reply yes. Simple as that. That`s how I see my product and opportunity. I just keep following up, planting the seed until an opportunity comes to present my story and/or the product.

If you plant the seed and keep watering it, it will grow. However, if you ignore and stop watering it, it will die. The same concept applies in your business. If you keep investing time into it, your business will grow. Ignore it or walk away and your business will die. You have to keep going and nourishing your relationships with value. No one wants to talk about business all the time; it gets old. Have the mindset to start building relationships because you truly want to connect. The business opportunity will come, but if you are always pushing and asking, you may jeopardize and push a relationship away.

Rob's Notes: Can I just say amen! I always say I don`t strive to be disliked but as long as I do my best, I am ok being disliked. Niches to riches. If you try to be everything to everyone, you will be nothing to no one. Standout and be you to the people that matter most!

Be the Cheerleader

No great football game ever existed without a cheering section. I never want to step on anyone's toes or tell the team something different than what their leaders said. If they're running and doing great, I don't have that momentum to change. I want to be on the sidelines cheering them on. If you have a rock star, you don't want to get in their way. Instead, figure out what they need by being their biggest supporter. Some people reach a certain point and create their own systems and reinvent the wheel. That's great! Keep using what works for you. You don't have to go rogue just because you are a leader now.

One of the greatest attributes that will increase your wisdom is having a relationship with your leader. Over time, you'll find what they need and when they need you. It's good to know what each individual's needs are on a team. In fact, when you see the potential someone has but they don't see their light, you can't push it on them. Even though you see how amazing they are, if they don't want that recognition, then that's their choice. It's not for you to decide. Don't push too hard, or you may push a loyal customer or member away for good. Keep your people close. Get involved in their life. You'll miss people if you don't draw them in. We call these groups "orphans." Know where your orphan tree is so you can assist. Introduce people to different levels because you never know who connects better with other people's values. Again, this will expose your group to other like-minded individuals, which creates opportunities for everyone. Use what you have in your tree line and keep extending outward. Sometimes, we commonly miss personality matches that might not happen on their own when we don't include our upline. Be upfront when connecting people. Be professional and respectful on how others communicate in their network.

Every day in your life, your relationships are constantly changing. My aunt Kelly always says, "You are in a different season right now." Whether it`s family, business partners, or friends the season can change people. My life looks different now than it did six months ago. Be willing to be flexible in seeing how your relationships can help support and uplift you through your seasons.

Author: Shanon Melynk

- Seven-figure earner in her business career.

- International Best Selling Co-author.

- Specializes in online marketing.

- In 2019, she became a top 25 Power Ranker in North America.

- Branding coach, a trainer, a speaker, and a travel addict.

- Fiercely passionate about people authentically achieving their dreams.

- Proud momma to her two favorite human beings in the whole world, Mike and Maddy.

- She exemplifies the phrase "conscious entrepreneur"...someone who takes massive responsibility for their life and results, someone who is growth obsessed and continues to become the highest version of themselves. They deeply care about self, others and the planet. They are here to live a life of freedom, money and impact, and to leave this world a better place.

- While the rest of the world was struggling with layoffs and isolation, she was winning and changing lives with automation, systems, and training programs...everyone wants to work from home with EASE and FLOW!

"The reason we work ONLINE is so that we can go anywhere OFFLINE... that's LIVING!

For the most part, I grew up on a very humble farm. The power was off more than it was on and the phone was disconnected more than it was connected. It was a life altering experience working with our cattle and horses. We trained them, broke them, and showed them. I learned so much about animals that no one should ever have to learn. My upbringing brought me a sense of gratitude while teaching me the value of patience. My life lessons taught me about patience, ethics and how to overcome adversity. As they say, what does not kill you makes you stronger. What I learned on the farm made me successful in my entrepreneurial career. I not only care about people, but I`m strong minded, driven and open to learning. In fact, I thrive on learning and being better today than I was yesterday.

Every day after school, I remember coming home and dreaming about being older and inspiring millions of people.. I still get teary-eyed thinking about how much of a dreamer I was even then. To be honest, I knew I wanted to get involved in a business but didn`t know anything about it. I had no idea how to be an entrepreneur and didn`t even know what that word meant.

Closing the Sale

Closing the sale isn`t complicated. For instance, we were at a corporate event and one of the owners had his Ferrari there. A girl on our team asked him if she could drive his car. He told her yes and surprisingly, let her drive his prized Ferrari. It was such a huge aha moment for me. All she did was genuinely ask! You have to be brave enough to ask for what you want. Most people aren`t brave to ask for the sale. It`s a three-letter word. What`s the worst that can happen? You get a no? If so, then that`s fine. What if you get a "yes" the next time around? The point is to always be following up. It is a continual follow-up even after the sale. Always be asking yourself when the next perfect time to follow up is. We have to be constantly building a relationship and asking for what we want. Ask, ask, ask! I let people know that my business is going to grow with or without them. We let them know that the business is successful if you put in the work. Be genuine and authentic with your clients. Provide them value. It`s important to ask but you have to keep the conversation going before and after the deal closes.

To be candid, people don`t know what you have to offer until you spark the conversation. Before the approach, figure out how your product or service aligns with the prospect. Again, ask! I am blessed that our online business is fully automated and I do attraction marketing, so I attract people who are in alignment with my core values. I send them links to watch videos and they learn simple duplication. Imagine that I never have to explain ingredients or products. We market high ticket items with high commissions and everyone sees the value in this compared to low ticket items and low commissions. It`s working in huge ways. All I have to do is be my authentic self through social media attraction marketing and build relationships. Someone else even closes our sales, you read that right. It`s so fun and refreshing.

Follow up with your people.

Someone asked me how I became a seven-figure earner in my career. I told them it was from consistently following up. It`s a practice skill to learn and it wasn`t something I was good at before. A "no" today doesn`t mean it`s a "no" tomorrow, next week, or in a couple of months or even years. Continue to follow up and ask. When you practice, make sure to follow up in a respectful manner. Be considerate of people`s time. Always reference people by name and send them birthday wishes, audio messages are my favorite. It`s so important to show that you authentically care.

When consulting your customers, ask them questions and help them figure out how you can be a solution provider for them. What problem do they have? How can you solve it? Show them how beneficial your solution can be to them and their family. In addition, have a great story to share so they can relate to you. Find out exactly what they want and why they need your product. Figure out how much time they`re willing to invest. When asking questions, it opens up the idea of commitment. Everyone wants to dream but not everyone is willing to put in the work if you don`t show them a vision.

> **Rob's Notes:** A mentor who has made over 30 million dollars once told me, "no asky ... no getty." Sure, these are made up words, but this has stuck with me for 13 years. Shanon became a seven-figure earner for many good, convincing reasons. One of the main reasons was because she asked! So many of us are scared to do this. By not asking we already assume the worst-case scenario on the most likely outcome of a "no." Get focused on this business! Find out what everyone`s talking about, visit www.sperrybonus.com for my top

eight income producing activities. It`s 100% free and will provide you the focus you need to crush your business. I can tell you Shanon practices what she preaches. If there is something that she needs help with, she always asks me in a loving, bold way. She knows what she wants and asks for it! As Nike says, "Just do it!"

Care Enough to Show Up

While looking at relationships, we notice some individuals don`t take the time to build them. Their only intent is the quick and immediate sale. Nine out of 10 messages in my inbox are about people trying to sell me something. I don`t see any signs of relationship building in these messages. Only a flat-out cold sale!

One afternoon, I had this woman consistently messaging me on Instagram. I finally responded, and she vomited all over me about her company and products. She had no interest in my well-being nor any idea what I`m looking for. It was a sad moment because I truly wanted to get to know her, but she cut off any form of relationship-building with her approach.

Showing up in the social media world can be our biggest asset or our biggest downfall. We all need human connection, whether it`s online or face to face. It`s something that people crave and at times, it is hard to come by. If you deeply care about people like you, it`s important to have some conversations with them from time to time. It could be about their relationship, their family, or their work. Make it personal and make it matter. Keep in mind relationships are building blocks. In reality if you really want to know what true hustlers eat, breathe and sleep, it`s the fundamentals of building worthwhile relationships. Afterall, you are the top 5 people in your circle, so always strive to level up.

You don`t need to tell your prospects about what you do right away, but you can if the timing is right. In fact, wait for the conversation to flow. Keep in mind some individuals don`t have others in their lives that genuinely care about them or their families. If it helps, be family- oriented with your client. One of the reasons I have attached myself to Rob Sperry is because he cares so much. You don`t have to prove you`re some rockstar millionaire to him. Wealthy or not, he cares and has the desire to lead others. This shows this industry is about having compassion for others. They say it`s better to buy from people you know, love, and trust, but also from those who want to get to know your story. One of the ways I show I care is by sending personal hand-written birthday or Christmas cards. Other times, I`ll call someone out of the blue, check in or send a quick text to see how they`re doing. The point is to take the time to care, show kindness and compassion always.

Have a goal in mind to build your avatar. What I mean is create a list of characteristics about your ideal customer. Be intuitive and find the right people that fit your avatar. Not everyone wants what we have. You have to know who you want to work with. We`re looking for soulful, conscious, good-hearted people who are passionate about inspiring change. As you continue to grow and learn, you`ll start to attract stronger like-minded people who fit your avatar. This is when the fun part of your journey begins!

Rob's Notes: Sometimes we tend to make things way too complicated! Yes of course we want to approach others and there are many ways to do so. Here is the solution, and Shanon said it perfectly. "Care enough to take the time and have a conversation." Shanon makes it simple and takes action! Don`t be the person that waits for months before you follow up with a prospect the second time around. Imagine being in the prospect`s shoes. Follow up with them in a timely manner and see when they want to be reached out to.

Know What works

It's fortunate we live in a technology-driven world that binds us globally. However, when COVID-19 came knocking at our doors, it confined us to isolation but allowed working from home to be more applicable than ever. With that said, I'm passionate about attraction marketing and the multiple streams of income that come along with it. That's why I partnered with a community involved in automation, systems, and training. It then becomes our obligation to plug prospects into this vital network. I've never seen anything like this in the last 10 years of my career. Now I see affiliates winning and crushing their business because these systems work. Imagine that. As a member, all you have to do is plug your prospects into a system that's already automated. Let the technology work for you and your team.

Also imagine being in an environment where building an audience requires being your authentic self. That's exactly what we do. For example, if you're a stay-at-home mom, then you build your audience around other moms, those you know directly or in your sphere of influence online. If you're a doctor or a nurse, then build your audience around those in your field. When you build your business around like-minded people, it's easy to construct your avatar since you all share the same professions. It will make your tribe more connected and engaged with each other while your sales volume increases.

What I love the most is organizing weekly zoom meetings online, you read that right, I never have to do home launches or weekly hotel meetings. The action takes place online and that's when the fun begins and everything will start to align. When everything is aligned, you feel whole and interconnected with your team. Make sure to bring a positive mindset when in these meetings. Life is always happening in our favor and creates lessons for us that we can share.

One thing I absolutely love about building a presence online is the value we add in our webinars. This helps us attract more prospects. In previous workshops, we educated teams not only about how to build online but make tools available to any team member who needs guidance in setting up their own webinars. Having the right tools proves effective and everyone wins when they can utilize these tools and convert them into skills to build their online presence. Part of my training program also comes with required reading guides and audiobooks that really help my affiliates, such as Rob Sperry`s books. I`m a huge advocate of books, especially audiobooks. They`re convenient to use when driving on the road, working out in the gym, preparing a meal, or cleaning the house. Today, we live in a world where educational resources are easily available and accessible online.

To all my teams, they know my integrity very well and understand how much I value their education. I`m grateful to everyone and appreciate their journeys. The opportunity to make seven plus figures is out there. You just have to make the right choices.

Grow on your Own

As you journey through life, it`s common to experience personal growth. In fact, you have to be the one to grow first. When your team sees this, they`ll duplicate your steps. It`s all about your personal development game and becoming the best version you can be. I always emphasize all parts of my story. If you think sharing your story doesn`t matter, think again. Your tribe will be more prone to connect with you when you share. Like millions of other people, I`m a person who`s tried and failed and kept trying until I got it right. I`m someone who grew up with nothing more than hand-made clothes. Always tell your personal stories so people know the real you. It`s not only about your product. Always remember where you came from, but don`t stay in the past. Be willing to put in the work to grow.

I know we can change how we view sales. In order to do that, we have to help people globally because there are people out there that matter and want to succeed. When you educate the world and help the right people, you can`t help but feel obligated to become a leader, someone who attracts a higher vibration frequency. Let`s help people see the positive changes they wish to see. Utilize the tools in this system to be the best version of yourself. When this happens, we all rise to the top!

Rob's Notes: Shanon is awesome because she genuinely cares! She loves her team. She loves on everyone. I can`t say this enough! Become the person you would want to recruit!

Author: Heidi Snider Kauffman

- Professional equestrian athlete and coach for over 23 years.

- Has worked part time in network marketing for the past five and a half years.

- Published Author of "With Sight Comes Power."

- Produced thousands of team members.

- Over $200,000 in personal sales.

- Wife and a mother of three.

- Builds winning teams online and offline.

- During the start of the pandemic in March of 2020, Heidi and her team recruited 90 new reps in one day.

"Simplicity is the ultimate sophistication."

- Leonardo Da Vinci

This is one of the best businesses to get into. The industry has changed me as a person and made me more positive, flexible, and creative. It has put me in situations where I had to figure things out more practically and diplomatically. I love network marketing; it really is something anyone can learn to do well. It gives you an opportunity to change hundreds of thousands of people`s lives for the better.

In January of 2015, I was burned out and exhausted. I was a typical mom figuring out how I was going to get the energy to work more. I needed to make more money and my biggest problem at the time were the expenses at my horse farm. There was always more month than there was money. The horse business was in a down cycle, as was my health. I was in the middle of a MS relapse. I was experiencing a physical, financial and emotional rock bottom. One evening, I was laying on the floor, hiding from my family, scrolling on Facebook trying to find a cat video to make me laugh. I saw a friend post a picture with her network marketing product. Surprisingly, she looked happy and healthy! She hadn`t looked that way in a long time. I wanted that for myself. I wondered, could this be the way for me to get my health and energy back on track and make a little money at the same time? To tell you the truth, this wasn`t really something I was looking for. I signed up and figured I would go for the first bonus. When I hit that first goal, I realized I joined a solid company that had an amazing product that worked for its customers.

When I saw this vision of what this industry could do for someone willing to put in the consistent daily effort, I knew I had to run with it.

Keep it Simple

To train horses, who have the mentality of a five-year-old, it has to be simple and consistent. To have a big team follow a system, it has to be simple. Your recruiting map must also be simple. You know exactly how your new teammate will be making his or her first sale, and that`s probably going to be with someone close to them. When that happens, celebrate their success, connect them to the tools your company or team offer, and make sure to reach out to them and follow up. Keep in mind, the very first post on social media is something interesting that draws people in, asks questions, makes comments and likes. Or it could be a live stream about what you`re doing throughout that day. "Today I got up and tackled my day like a boss. I haven`t felt this good in ages!"

Ultimately, I create many posts on social media that aren`t product or company specific. In fact, every week I do a Monday Motivation Facebook live stream with my daughter. People get a chance to see us together. It`s a big risk to put a nine-year-old on video, but over time, she`s grown to be an amazing speaker on camera. Our viewers love to see and hear her share her insights.

When I first started in network marketing, I was shy about posting pictures on social media. I found out the more I posted, the more valuable my content was to my viewers. I would have potential team members say, "I can never do what you do" or "I can`t be like you." My reply was, "The world has enough people like me; what it needs is more people like you!" In other words, the audience you attract are the ones that will relate to you. You`ll see how everyone inspires each other to become leaders. That`s what makes social media so much fun!

I teach time management and consistency to my team. You can move mountains with 20-30 min of focused effort 2-3x per day. Consistent daily effort will increase your and your teams recruiting and sales. Daily activities such as reaching out, building connections and follow ups are the key to building long lasting success.

Rob's Notes: Successful people just do the basics better. All of us want the secret and the shortcut. I've worked with Heidi for over six months and seen how she simplifies everything. To be a great leader requires continued recruiting inside your team. You must keep the process simple. Too many distributors complicate simple actions that create "analysis paralysis." Don't over complicate your business!

Be Visible

Becoming visible is challenging for a lot of people. To be prosperous in this way, people have to be able to find you through attraction marketing. When you`re visible, they`ll be keen to know who you are. In other words, put yourself out there! Attend a party, go to a luncheon or the food marketplace. Getting that face to face interaction is crucial to the success of your business. Stand out; be willing to be visible to your community.

Wherever I go, I`m conscious about where I spend my time. Twice a month, I attend a women`s networking luncheon and once a week, I am at a networking luncheon for both men and women. You`ll be surprised how many people you`ll come across at noon that want to do something different than what they are currently doing. If you come across too aggressive, they won`t show interest, but if you take time to get to know your prospect, they`ll be interested in learning more about what you do. These networking groups at luncheons can be very welcoming. Enjoy lunch and be yourself when you are connecting with other networkers over a delicious meal. That`s how some of the best friendships and businesses partnerships start.

One day I was coming home from a networking marketing event in Las Vegas, and a woman asked me if I was interested in taking a look at some of her products in a FB message. Long story short, when I found out she was on my team I was a bit embarrassed because someone else reached out to her before I did. She was in my contact list, and we were acquaintances, but not close. Still, I knew she would be a good fit. This shows how robust network marketing can be. It gave me relief to know my recruiting skills paid off and were being duplicated by a simple reach out. What a small world we live in!

Allow it to be their Idea

When you ask the right questions, customers will feel greater comfort and excitement in buying your product, especially when they know you`re getting to know them and are focused on meeting their needs. As the recruiter, this is a good time to see if they would be a good fit for your company. When you hear their story and find ways to solve their problems, they`ll feel more connected to you. If the conversation continues, I`ll ask them, "Where do you see yourself in the next five years? What is on your bucket list that you haven`t been able to do yet? What seems so far out there you haven`t even seen it as an option? "What would it take for you to step out of your comfort zone?" Nine out of ten people say more money would bring them out of their safety zone. These connecting then recruiting strategies work! As this happens, their curiosity will start to surface, which will make them more open and your product/opportunity more presentable. If you focus on solving a problem (lack of personal or family time, money, vacation, too much stress, etc..), you allow your potential recruit to see how your team is a good fit.

Picture this. You are a new recruit, excited and want to shout it out from the top of your lungs. Everyone`s excitement level is at different places. Find out where those close to you are in their excitement by saying "I am excited about xyz, let`s do this together!" Then you can ask them if they want any more info. If they show a 4+ interest on a one to 10 scale, provide them with some info or a quick video, whatever tool your company or team`s system recommends.

Rob's Notes: This is a relationship-type business. Yes, each one of you has different styles and personalities. Some of you may be building your business more online while others more offline. Some of you may not want to ever meet with anyone, but don`t lose sight of the main principle here. Once someone has committed to your business, remember this business is all about interaction. Creating connections are key to opening up new cultural relationships and, with that, more clients. Successful people have challenges like everyone else, but they`re willing to do what it takes because their purpose and vision are greater than the objections that come their way.

The Connection Group

As mentioned before, one of the biggest challenges with communication in network marketing is with recruitment. People are always wanting to organize and train their teams in different ways. This is fine, but they need to make sure they have a good interconnected communication system in place. In other words, you want your teammates to have the ability to connect with leadership should something happen to you or if they need more help. Connection is key. This is where leaders need to connect new recruits to someone who can assist their teams. For me that`s a trusted upline who wants to see my team win. I`ve set up the same layers of leadership within my team so they can continue duplication without me being there 24/7 and allowing me to continue to recruit more team members. I give credit to my mentor leaders in explaining how this process works.

For the most part I have a core rank that I want my members to reach. Once they hit that rank, I let them know they are now the leader of that team, and I go. When a team is limited by strict leadership, they can`t get all the information and connections that they need. Odds are anyone who is limiting their team wants to be seen as the only reliable one to come too. One night, my dad was in the hospital, and I let everyone know I wasn`t going to be available for a day or two. I gave my team a couple key leadership contacts to reach out to while I was absent. The idea is to make the connections now. The more you connect, the easier it is to have a duplication process in place for your team to last through the next generation of team members.

I have found the best connections you can make are with credible experts, trainers, and leaders. When you think you don`t need to learn anymore, you`ll absolutely fall flat. At times, I felt like I was struggling and needed more training. I needed to talk to people who`ve been in the business for 10 to 20 years. When I felt stuck, I wanted to find people who really believed in this business. Those were the kind of connections I was seeking. When I found Rob Sperry, he changed the way I looked at my goals with a new profound belief.

With my horse training farm, I would bring in other top coaches and judges to train my students once a month in the off season. We call these weekend events clinics. With Rob, I saw how he performed with his masterminds. Both clinics and masterminds provided intensive quality training in a short amount of time. With Rob`s masterminds, you get to learn a variety of business modules and ideas in a short amount of time. I appreciate Rob. He`s one of the best teachers out there. He teaches us not only to be better professionals but well-rounded industry leaders.

Rob's Notes: I`ve had the opportunity to coach Heidi, and she`s the real deal! Heidi gives an example on why keeping things simple is crucial to all aspects of your business. In the book *The Influencer*, the author mentions two questions everyone asks themselves in decision making. One, can I do what you are doing and two, is it worth it? These two questions are simple and profound. When you make your invite a complicated process to understand, it`ll make prospects hesitant about joining. Even though you want to appear as the expert when recruiting, it`s ok to have other teachers step in and exemplify how other experts run the business. Follow the K.I.S.S. strategy. Keep It Simple Stupid.

Author: Karla Neal Pierce

- Three-time six figure earner.

- Team of over 54,000 members

- Over 50 elite leaders in my downline.

- 5th person in the company to reach my current rank.

- First person to hit two elite ranks in consecutive months.

- 4.5 years in the network marketing industry.

- The team averages ten million in retail sales monthly.

- First African American to reach five different company ranks and three different company milestones.

- In the top 0.1% in leadership and product sales out of 350,000 consultants.

- Personally recruited 185 business partners.

"Your grind has to match your goals. Walk it like you talk it."

To obtain results, you must have a goal, organization and direction. I have daily methods of operation (DMO) in place that guide me through each day. Utilizing my DMO`s keeps me on task and provides a benchmark that allows me to measure my success. This is critical for me. For example, effectively communicating with my team is crucial and growing my team is vital.

Daily, I have a set number of people that I speak with, which include potential business owners, customer follow-ups and my team members. I also create daily challenges for my team. These challenges amass meaningful results in addition to generating synergy, excitement and motivation.

Prior to creating/announcing challenges you must have a budget in place, know what excites your team members, project outcomes, establish a timeline, identify who can participate and you absolutely must be organized. Once the challenge is set up, prepare for the follow-up. Yes, part of implementing a challenge is the follow-up. The lack of follow up happens far too often in this industry, therefore be prepared for the follow up and have fun with your challenge. Challenges should always produce meaningful results. I never start a challenge in my business without having the end result in mind. The aforementioned are examples of just two of my DMO`s!

Set yourself up for success! Engagement, Engagement, Engagement! Plugging in and engaging are fundamental components of success. Create a platform of education and motivation and utilize your personally designed challenges to attain engagement. There is an array of best practices, key business tools, and systems pertaining to your industry that are vital to growth and success. Capitalize on your challenges to continuously teach and show people how to become successful in their business. Most importantly, acknowledge and celebrate "every" victory!

Knowledge, consistency and follow-up matter. Know and understand your product. As you create challenges, think holistically. Create fun interactive challenges that teach people the business, the importance of repetition, and the importance of follow-up. This builds confidence. In our industry, we share the opportunity, recruit or build by talking to everyone. When people are confident, they understand the art of controlling a conversation by asking questions and the importance of "hearing" responses. Create a mentorship program and pair team members with an accountability partner to create goals and execution. Once confident, the number of daily contacts increase which insure the need and desire for immediate follow-up.

To obtain a productive follow-up with a prospect, I narrow down a convenient time for them. If this means, I need to adjust my schedule to accommodate the prospect then I make the necessary modifications. I am persistent and consistent with follow-up as I understand it is important to the life and growth of my business.

Personally, I go hard every single day with follow-up as it is one of my DMO`s. This consistency is one of the main reasons why I am a top recruiter and earner today. I like the quality of my life and I work hard to maintain it. Implement a system and challenge yourself to improve your skills daily! Learn how to follow up.

> **Rob's Notes:** Discipline is the mother of being consistent. Show me your minimum goals, what your habits are, and I`ll show you the future. Too many network marketers keep looking for the shortcut. They`re unwilling to follow through with hundred percent effort. Which means they may be left with zero success.

Invest in the Success of Others

I have an annual set budget to execute challenges. Please note; some challenges are less expensive than others and some challenges do not warrant a prize. In fact, I often issue challenges on our mentoring calls. Keep in mind, that the best prize is the production activity that comes out of the challenge.

I adore this business! Thus far, this has been an amazing journey. It is a continuous growth process. As a leader, I want everyone to win and it`s often hard to differentiate when you are doing too much for your team and when it`s best to step aside and allow them to figure things out independently. Get to know your team members` motivations.

A while back I met a wonderful team member that was excited about the daily challenges. I noticed her work production and recognized her on my group page. She and several of her team members sent me a message stating, "It was such an honor that you recognized us!" Recognition really makes a difference. Recognizing people and mentioning them in your story is impactful. I love seeing the effect it has on others.

In general, challenges are activity-driven, and garner results. If team members consistently partake in the activities/challenges; results are sure to follow. One of my most recent challenges has been asking my business partners to "show me their sales." I wanted to see how much they were selling. It is extremely important to ensure daily growth. If they are selling products daily, they are moving their business forward. The highest sales volume may receive anything from a gift card to a tablet. The best part about team challenges is the trickle-down effect that can occur. Not only do team members host challenges for their teams but they also facilitate challenges on Social Media when marketing their products. The social media challenges have broadened their customer base and access to potential business partners. Challenges are a win for all!

I love thriving in this industry because you`re compensated and recognized for doing what you enjoy. I love the flexibility and the ability to work from home. This business gives me the opportunity to not only help my family but others as well. Recently, I purchased my dream home with no cosigner. It was such a blessing. My story gives hope to other single and divorced women. Remain faithful, focus, take action, and amazing can happen.

Be Happy and Smile

When I talk to anyone, no one is safe! If they give me a compliment, it`s an opportunity to talk to them about my business. I believe that everyone should be part of a direct sales or network marketing company. It`s a great way to reach out to others, formulate teams, and make good money. I share this industry with everybody, and I don`t prejudge anyone. The person I`m talking to may not be a rock-star, but they might lead me to one. Everyone is significant. In addition, smiling is a huge part of recruiting and winning! When you smile, people feel positive energy and want to be part of your excitement and fun. Be willing to spread your joy and smile with everyone.

I prefer recruiting in person. People get to see more of my personality and get a glimpse of who I am. I`m not a big "join my team" person. I only show people what I`m doing and the success of my team. Everyone wants to be part of success. Create a challenge surrounding meeting new people. Apply your creativity and consider the skills that your team will learn from the challenge never mind the confidence gained by your team members.

I often write and plan ideas in my notebook. I write down phrases like "wearing a tan shirt and glasses" or "living in the pacific time zone." These notes serve as a memory jogger. When I meet potential business partners or customers, I take notes on our conversation and interaction and use the information during our follow-up. Once I recruited a woman who was wearing a purple shirt. When I followed up with her, I mentioned how I liked her purple shirt and how great it looked on her! To this day, we joke about her glamorous purple shirt.

Another woman I recruited came through a customer of mine. The woman stated to my customer that she was thinking of signing up with the company. My customer told her, "You have to sign up with Karla. She`s the best!" I gave my customer such great service that she referred me to a friend. Be personable and provide people with Nordstrom customer service! Customer service is very important in this industry. It is necessary to apply this skill set in person and with online interactions. Be intentional about providing an amazing experience to your customers; which causes repeat business.

Remember, do not make recruiting difficult. Do not prejudge or make assumptions. Talk to everyone as if they need to join you on this journey. When I started, no one was off limits. I spoke to everyone and I always asked for referrals. A successful approach I used was to ask a customer or potential business partner to think of people who would benefit from a new business or product. Implementing this strategy takes skill, which allowed me to recruit 185 affiliates. Never stop recruiting, always build even if your team has enormous growth, keep building! My team is phenomenal; I have people all over the country. Everyone can do well in this industry. The choice is yours.

I am a Founder of a nonprofit organization called "Karla Kares." The primary mission of Karla Kares is to help underserved youth obtain access to resources needed throughout college. I believe in giving back to my community. I`m incredibly thankful that my business success allows me to do so. To God be the Glory!

> **Rob's Notes:** Now you know! You just read Karla`s chapter on why she`s successful with the energy she brings when she steps into the room. Challenge yourself to set a daily method of operations that works for you. Challenge yourself to be accountable to your DMO with consistent effort. In network marketing you have no boss. You`re your own boss, and it`s vital to always stay focused.

Author: Jessica Matney

- Team has sold over $16 million in product in 2.5 years.

- Produced 3322 team members.

- Three-time conference speaker.

- Corporate appointed regional trainer.

- Incentive trip earner.

- Founding member of the company.

- Reached the highest paid level in the compensation plan structure.

- Earned Elite Presidential Title with only 67 other stylists.

"It's not who you think you are that holds you back, it's who you think you're not."

- Denis Waitley

I remember exactly how I felt when I realized I lost my whole identity. To my sphere of influence, I was known as the military wife or my children`s mother. My whole life revolved around waking up, taking care of everyone else, then going to bed to only repeat it again the next day.

What no one knew was I endured extensive abuse behind closed doors and felt no way out of this cycle of chaos and depression. To be honest, I didn`t realize what I was going through until the worst hit. I was so disconnected from myself that I couldn`t remember what my favorite color was! Sounds silly, but it was true. I couldn`t remember my favorite color, who goes through that? For a period of time, I realized my lifestyle wasn`t stable and I was hurting myself emotionally by staying stagnant. I needed to change, and I had two choices. I could continue living in my dark existence or take steps to become a greater version of myself. I remember sitting down on the couch late one night and committing to myself that I would start a new path the next morning.

The very next day, I received a call from a woman who was offering me the opportunity to start a new business. We would be the first members of a new company that would be launching two months later. My initial reaction was "this is ridiculous." However, I remembered the commitment I had made to myself, and the more I thought about it, the more I realized this could be exactly what I needed. The following day, I took a leap and joined this new company and said yes to network marketing. I give credit to my sponsor who helped me make the breakthrough. This was an opportunity for change, and I was so blessed I received that phone call. Luckily, we had those two months to prepare. There I found myself sitting alone thinking about the future. I asked myself, "Why would anyone want to join me on this journey?" and "What sets me apart from everyone else?"

Rob's Notes: Let`s put this in perspective. I recently introduced Jessica as a featured speaker at my event in Australia. I spoke about how much she produced in sales volume ever since she started. Thirteen million dollars in sales volume! Are you kidding me? This was her third network marketing company. Remember, she was in a very dark place and had her doubts and fears. Some of you may be rolling your eyes thinking, "How does this apply to me?" This is a life-changing story-telling business. Facts and stories speak for themselves. Sometimes, we think we don`t need to hear other people`s stories, but we all need to understand the value behind people`s stories in order to bring coherence to our own beliefs! Jessica shows that anyone can do this business, that anyone who takes deliberate action can make it possible. Remember, it doesn`t happen overnight. You need to focus on learning, be truthful, and have integrity throughout the whole process.

That`s when I decided I would breathe life into people. I would lead with friendship, understanding, and acceptance rather than my product or compensation plan. That`s what I had needed for so long. I couldn`t be the only person on the planet who wanted to be seen and encouraged. I ran with this tactic moving forward.

Though I was starting a new business, I didn`t want anyone to feel like a number. I wanted everyone to feel appreciated and worthy of more. When we treat everyone as friends (first) rather than by profession, it makes communication easier, and the willingness to work harder increases. Motivation and positivity will become clearer. It will allow others to dream higher and aim bigger. Friends first, leadership second. When I have shared about my past, I have opened the door for others to share. More peers confirmed they felt the same way, and by accepting them as who they are, I helped build their confidence and breathed life back into them.

I know there are people who need more in life but don`t have the support. By being open and relatable, you can become the comfort others need in order to find their confidence. There`s joy in witnessing people realize they deserve positivity and greatness. It`s one of the most rewarding things to see. Yes, I sell a product, but it`s so much more than that!

Network marketing has given me the ability to help my peers in any situation. It fuels me to be their friend. I`ve opened my home, given out my phone number and made myself available to anyone who needs support. I teach my team these strategies so they can help their friends out, as well. This is why I have one of the strongest teams in my company. Our morale is always high, the atmosphere uplifting, and there`s always a desired willingness to show up.

Rob's Notes: Jessica found a way to be her blunt authentic self! We saw how vulnerable she was and changed her focus to help others. She provided herself with a cosmic towering vision. She didn`t allow short term rejections to prevent her from achieving her long-term goals.

"Hey Girl!"

Avoid sending that "hey girl" message! If we`re going to change the world with network marketing and friendship, then be a friend. When you see your friend receiving a promotion, congratulate them. When you see someone buy a new home, congratulate them. Take a look at your prospect`s social media feed, get to know them through their posts, spend time looking at their Facebook page, find what similar pages you like, and ask them questions! Eventually, they may show curiosity and ask what you do. This is when you can tell them about your business. Be a friend first, and the opportunities you want to share will come after.

In addition, it`s always significant to keep your face in front of your team. Avoid that 'hey girl` message once a month to see if they`re going to get anymore sales. Instead, create fun days by inviting them to events. Again, if we mold the friendship first, then business opportunities will be more presentable. Take time to see that you`re creating a warm welcoming culture. Take ownership with good intentions.

To be frank, before I started this business, I had no idea how to recruit. Before our company`s launch, none of us knew what to do. We jumped right in without training or guidance. One early morning, my sponsor and I sat down and talked about how we wanted to be recruited. What would it take us to say "yes!" We put ourselves in the customer`s shoes and imagined how a recruiter would approach us. Role playing was very essential and opened up many diverse avenues to learn more. When you know what a customer is struggling with, listen, really listen. Lend them your ear and build rapport. The business will naturally come second.

Positive Community

I had many visions about how I wanted my team, community, and culture to be like. This doesn't happen overnight. This is where reaching out to your community helps. Think about it. If your community is already engaged with events, find out what their culture is like. It helps to know more!

While in San Antonio, Texas, at a conference, a leader approached and asked if we could talk. She needed advice on a specific situation, and wanted my advice on how I would handle it. Her question was about team issues and self-awareness, and I gave her a cut and dry answer. She said, "how do you do that? How have you grown to be that person that can just cut off negativity?" For me it's easy, I just won't allow drama or negativity to flourish in any part of my life, especially business.

When I returned home, another leader called to ask how I bring balance to my team. She was very impressed to see no negative comments on my team's page. To be direct, it's simple. If there's ever a problem you encounter, go to your leader first. Never talk about it with your team or the people you recruit. I always tell my team to reach out to me directly via call, text, or email. The team community is not the place for negativity, bad-mouthing, and discouragement. If they feel anything of this nature, I let them know to reach out.

A friend recently posted a quote on Facebook that read, "Fear creates fear." When I first read it, I laughed and thought how could you create something if it already existed? Then I realized that was a perfect quote for leadership. As a leader, it's my duty to ensure I share information to my team in a way that doesn`t instill fear or panic. It`s the simplest, smallest, negative comments that can change the energy in an unforgiving way. Don`t plant a bad seed. Furthermore, never let your team see when you`re upset. This kind of energy will make your team feel on edge. If your team is repeatedly exposed to negative energy, members will start to fall apart. This results in a chain reaction where other members will leave your group and you may have to build from the bottom up.

One of my favorite things to do is spend time face to face with local team members. I try to invite different people each time so it`s not the same crowd. I like to see what kind of energy people bring to others. In fact, anytime we do something as a group we post it on social media so everyone can see the fun! Recently, we had an "ugly sweater" day where we pick out ugly outfits for each other from a thrift store. We wore them to lunch and around downtown-it was a blast! I also invited local team members who haven`t been able to attend prior functions. I wanted them to build bonds within the local team community. One of the ladies that attended made a post later about our "ugly sweater" day. In the post she wrote how she felt she belonged, was seen, recognized, and accepted. She also shared that she had been longing for bonds with friends for many years, and that day changed her life. When I saw her post, I couldn`t hold back my tears. This is exactly what network marketing is all about. I want you to feel like you belong!

Rob's Notes: The real financial benefit behind the business is where the money is. But what does that mean? It means you must multiply the numbers in your business. Jessica created a culture that was more valuable than her products and commissions. She created a culture that new people wanted to be a part of when they were not making much money and had no one there for support.

Fall Back and Follow Up

Fall back and follow up. This doesn't have to be strictly between you and your prospects. Tap into your team and follow up with people you recruited days, weeks, and months ago, especially with those you've lost touch. When you create a vast community that is connected to everyone, it'll provide you comfort knowing others are part of an alliance. I remind my team of this often and savor reaching out to new members well. Often, I'll dive further into my database and reach out to someone I haven't met yet. Here's a pro tip, your next powerhouse team member may be 20 levels below you. Reach out to them; you'll find out if they're progressing slowly or moving full steam ahead in their business. Help them pinpoint both their biggest strengths and weaknesses. You don't know what may have changed in a person's life over a prolonged period of time. They may be experiencing something you're an expert at, and you can help them bridge that gap.

When you follow up and create bonds with your team, you create space for them to share with their friends. You're creating a place where people feel great about referring their friends to join. You can share a good experience or something you're grateful for. It doesn't always have to be about the product or the business. Open up the conversation with a go-getter! These strategies have helped me foster connections in a safe place for everyone to share.

One of the ways I challenge my group is by telling them to reach into their sphere of influence and find 10 people they don't know very well. I have them reach out to those individuals and text them, "Thanks for being here," and see what kind of response they get back.

My team has had a lot of success using this simple direct message. Sometimes the acknowledgement alone will make the greatest impact.

Be willing to do the small things consistently. It pays off leaving a pathway for greater commodities to come. It really isn`t about the product you have to offer, that`s just your vehicle. It`s about the lives you can change and the journey with which that vehicle takes you. I challenge you to find someone on your team you don`t know very well and take them out to dinner, have drinks with them, learn what makes them happy. Really start to make authentic connections. Keep the face to face interactions going. Share your genuine personality, and your reputation will steadily increase in a positive light.

Go For "No" Challenge!

This is by far my favorite challenge we`ve done! Everyone says the J months are the worst. January, June and July. At the end of December 2019, I created the "Go for No Challenge" for my team. In the first month, the mission was for everyone to go for 100 noes. Instantly, this challenge dramatically changed the dynamic of my team. But why was this challenge so much different than others? You see, I gave the team permission to fail. Everyone thought it would be so easy to get 100 noes, but even my shyest team members couldn`t do it. We were bombarded with mostly yeses!

I had a happy, healthy team before, but this challenge greatly improved morale. Recruiting increased, sales increased, and promotions were endless in January. At the end of the month, I randomly selected participants and rewarded them with incentives for working so hard. It`s important to recognize effort, not always the top producers.

The team loved this challenge and were so successful they wanted to do it the following month. Everyone realized they hadn`t put in enough effort earlier. Truth is, you can always do more to improve the productivity of your team! This challenge just made sense to me. What challenges have worked best for your team?

Be open to trying different tactics, try to stay adaptable to what curveballs life throws at you. Be available. Be understanding. Be open to change. Believe and encourage. You don`t have to be the best network marketer on the planet to be successful. Just be your authentic self, and never stop striving to be better tomorrow.

Author: Stacy Ziegler

- $32 million team volume.

- Joined network marketing spring of 2017.

- Top 20 team with company.

- Currently her team has over 5,000 members and has produced over 30 million in less than 3 years.

- Speaker, coach and trainer specializing in business math everyone can do.

"Do or Do Not. There is no try."

-Yoda

I used to be a habitual "kit napper." You know, the person that takes kits from the marketing conferences but never uses them after? In January 2017, I started with another network marketing business. I signed up excitedly, went to my sponsor and told them I was ready to learn. Her words haunted me, "Go and sell." That was it. That was my training, and I was frustrated.

I knew I had to sell but was hoping for some mentorship, some training or something real! Eventually I moved on to selling a ton, but at the end of the day, I didn't have any business training and was not learning how to run my business the way I wanted to.

After some time, I came across a new friend who introduced me to a different company. I told her about my background in photography. We talked about product pictures and what it took to launch a new company.

I quickly decided to sign up and it turned out I loved the product and the new company. I thought it would be another "kit nap" but my friend proved me wrong. Soon after we launched, I logged into my back office and saw my team had 152 people on it. My vision was brighter than ever. I remember the vivid moments with the other sponsor and the lack of training she provided. She left me in despair during a time I was trying to make a better life for my family. I knew nothing about how direct sales worked in network marketing. I knew I wanted to do my best in helping those 152 affiliates have the business they envisioned. I invested in learning how to support my team. I spent time getting to know them, and it was worth it. When you invest and get to know your team, you are investing in your business.

I love numbers. Math, data, and anything dealing with patterns fascinates me. When I studied business in college, it provided me with essential skills. However, with network marketing, I didn't know what numbers to track, how many people to contact, or where to get new leads. It raised questions about what I should be doing every day to grow as a business owner. I went with what I knew, studying books and learning everything I could to increase my knowledge about what successful marketers did to run a product line business.

I knew information systems and data analytics well, but the data from network marketing really interested me. I studied how business owners tracked their systems so that I could apply these concepts to my team.

Because I had such a love for numbers, it felt easy to find the data and create systems. I realized quickly that not everyone on my team was going to connect with the data and numbers. I had to find a way to make the data accessible to everyone. I figured out a way to make math and business analytics work for my team, and anyone else I shared this with. Giving your team power to take ownership in increasing recruiting conversion ratio is logical. When I`m not available, these platforms are available to all my team members on our group forum pages. The numbers are always there. When people know what to look for, it helps them feel like they are in the driver`s seat of their business.

Anyone who builds a business is eventually going to have a system on how to run their business. I not only created new systems, but I found systems that were already working and implemented them in network marketing. One of the systems I found that helped me recruit more in the business was the "Formula for Change" by Richard Beckhard and David Gleicher.

This formula helps us to understand different people and how likely they are to do network marketing. Can you imagine meeting with people and being able to know where they are at with their interest level? The Formula for Change helps determine if a new recruit will sign up and apply the work to be successful.

The formula looks like this:

$$D \times V \times P > R.$$

Dissatisfaction times vision times plan is greater than someone's resistance.

This is what it means. DISSATISFACTION times VISION times PLAN must be greater than someone's RESISTANCE. When meeting with a prospect you want to rate what their dissatisfaction level is between a 1-10. 1 is not at all, and 10 is very high. Then see where their vision of the future is at using the same scale. Next, check-in and see how easy your plan, new consultant training or daily method of operations are to follow for success. The last thing to check is how high is their resistance to change, the business, and network marketing. This will give you their numbers. The thing you want to watch for is if there are any zeros or ones on the dissatisfaction, vision, and plan side. If there is, that means that it is highly likely that this prospect won't work out.

The formula is helpful as we start to talk to people about the business, but understand that all of the numbers are not set. As we talk to our prospects we can help them increase their numbers and work the equation to their benefit.

Rob's Notes: You may think you're too introverted or extroverted. Perhaps you think you don't have the style or the personality. Stop making excuses. Throughout this book, you've read and will continue to read about many different styles and personalities. Your weakness is your hidden strength, but only if you allow it. My greatest fear was public speaking. I was awful at it for seven years. Public speaking is now my greatest strength and has allowed me to bond well with others.

We've seen the obstacles Stacy faced with different companies. She didn't have success until claiming responsibility for her capable strengths. She began to focus on finding solutions and finding them she did. She's literally one of the smartest people I've met. She is my go-to person for anything with technology. She's brilliant. In the next section Stacy will provide her formula for change to help take your recruiting business to another new level.

The Equation at Work

When recruiting, you have to find out what the prospect's dissatisfaction is. Dissatisfaction is something every person has. Talk to people to find their pain points, the things that are making them dissatisfied and what is making them think about network marketing or creating a business. Ultimately their dissatisfaction is not something you can change. Knowing their dissatisfaction is a way of helping to know how to best work with the recruit and see how you can help them solve their own dissatisfaction. Talk about their resistance because it will come innately from them.

If I am talking to someone and they say, "this is awesome, I am ready to go." I know that their resistance level is very low. If I am talking to someone and they are throwing up all the signs and signals that they are resistant to the business, network marketing, etc that means their resistance number is going to be high. Rate their resistance and put it into the Formula for Change.

This is how I work with recruiting. If I ever find that there is a one or zero on the left side of the equation, I know that it is never going to work and that they aren't willing to change. Their willingness to change and be successful in network marketing is not compatible. We can have discussions and find what's holding them back. Ultimately their dissatisfaction and resistance are something you can't change but only keep in mind when recruiting.

A side note: These are subjective numbers that I come up with. It not only helps me to see who to recruit, it also helps me to gauge what funnel the recruit will travel through once they sign up with me.

I worked with a woman that was living on a trust fund. She wanted to do something on her own, but her dissatisfaction with her life was low, and that meant her work ethic never showed up. Her resistance to work and change was greater than the rest of the equation. She could never get a vision of what was possible for herself either. She wasn`t dissatisfied with her life. It never happened. We gave her the steps for success through the daily method of operations, but she didn`t have the drive to work and make it happen.

Here is something I also look for in "The Equation for Change." Look at what the issue is, see what they are missing, and how you can incorporate it. If the change is gradual, then their incentive isn`t big enough to make the move. Their vision plays a significant aspect in how well they will do. Vision is what we can help people create.

Ask questions to see what people imagine their life could be. Ask questions to figure out why they would want that type of life. Be willing to walk them through a vision process to see what is possible. We can talk to people about what has changed in our life, we can show them what could be possible for them. We can paint a picture of financial freedom and time freedom. We can work with them on the vision, by painting the picture of our own.

People create their vision and we can provide the systems and numbers that show people how to be successful. Be consistent in talking about vision if you want positive changes in people`s lives. Be willing to share your vision of your future to be an example to others. Provide your team tools so you can create the vision and set their expectations. Great teams aren`t built in a month but rather in several months or years.

Make it simple to start a business. When starting and creating the "P", Action Plan, the steps need to be simple. We people start with our team, it is so simple. The first step says, "watch this video." You can`t get more simple than that.

Keep the steps so small and let people do it how they want to. It was such a small thing, but it builds huge foundations for people in their businesses. Get the steps to be small. Have a checklist for them. Have a checklist and tell your affiliates to take it one day at a time in understanding the video.

Occasionally, tell them, "Go watch this training and then get back to me with your questions." When I do this, it gives me the opportunity to see their commitment level in the beginning phase. I`ll tell them to come back and explain what their interest level is before moving forward. This puts them in a place of ownership since it`s ultimately their business. Make sure not to give too many steps. Make it as simple as possible. "Complete step one, then report back to me with your questions before we move on to step two." This attention to details shows how committed you are to your affiliates.

Some people in the business don`t know how to create Facebook groups, run an Instagram page, or how to log into a social media account. That`s ok, we can teach these skills. I make sure the administration tools are available. If I see someone engaging more than others, I`ll ask them "How do you think we can utilize this data?" I let them brainstorm and come up with new ways that work toward their advantage. I have them brainstorm and come up with a way to use the data to their advantage. For instance, in the example, I just used it could be beneficial to reach out to the person engaging the most with a thank you note and some product samples.

I also will teach my team how to run a Facebook group. I show them how to post, interact, and then engage. It`s their job to take notes and see how it`s done. When ready, they take over and put their own flavor into it. I help them apply the framework, show them how to do it, and they take over.

Some people that come on board may be resistant to change or hesitant to jump right in. They're the ones that sit back and watch what happens. You have to look at how to reach people that are a little more reluctant and resistant. You have to change your story and change your simple steps. There are always waves of a business cycle. You have to learn to ride the waves and how it played into the formula of change. This is where you work on their vision by outlining yours. Work on making your action steps simple. Make sure the resources are there.

> **Rob's Notes:** Good leaders have vision, but great leaders give vision. Great leaders are committed to showing up and not quitting. My entire book *The Game of Conquering* or at www.thegameofconquering.com talks about these great leaders. Stacy just gave you an exact formula for why people buy. There's one quote from here I want to emphasize, "The equation for change." Look at what the issue is, see what they're missing, and how you can guide them. Stacy is a top earner in the industry and understands how to ask the right questions while providing simple solutions. She gives clear vision to help her team get through the obstacles that come.

Use the Equation to Build the Story

Your leaders need to come to your own conclusions when making a decision. We use the formula for change to recruit and formulate the story. They are the Jedi. You are Yoda. You need to formulate the story and show them how to guide their members and point them in the right direction. Your recruit is the hero in their own story.

Formulate the picture and show them the way. One woman on my team is a nurse. She was always behind on her bills and didn`t know how she could make ends meet. One day, she saw her friend make a post about network marketing and she decided to go for it. She went from dissatisfaction to seeing a vision. She jumped into it, took the chance, and worked on the necessary steps to make her goals a reality.

Everyone has their own story and has a vision for their future, even if they don`t know it. Using the formula helps people start to see their vision. Using this formula helps them formulate their own story. When I bring someone on board, I always ask why they want to do it. I ask them how much time and brute effort they`re willing to put into this business.

Share your vision and story with others. It can be on social media, one on one, or reach out to your circles. Work on your story. Watch movies and dissect the story. See what makes a great storyline. Create a great storyline for your life. Use the formula to start to create the story. Have people create a story for themselves.

In my past, I had a job that very few people in the world will ever have. My job was something that I couldn`t talk to anyone about, and if I could, most people wouldn`t understand what I actually did for work. Regardless of what I did, or who I worked for, I always wanted to stay relatable to people. I didn`t want people to think that they needed to have a certain degree, or past, or work history to succeed in this business. ANYONE can do this business. Doesn`t matter who you are or what you do, you can by being relatable. Show them how they can make it happen. Walk them through the formula for change and create the story.

With attraction marketing, I highlight people on my team so I can relate them to other affiliates. It takes 20 exposures to sell something new. I make sure I`m exposing people to different stories so they can find the one relatable to them. Show them engaging stories about people`s transformations. It doesn`t have to be your story. When recruiting, I`m doing my best to make that connection with my potential prospect. Do your due diligence in being ready to collect good quality stories so you can relate them to other people.

The systems are there. Don`t find yourself saying you can`t or that you are confused by a system. Break it down and figure out how it is going to relate to you and help you find success in network marketing.

> **Rob's Notes:** In the case for all of these chapters, this one alone is something you could read time and time again. You could spend a whole year rereading this chapter and implementing these principles. You`ll find other successful teams using the same marketing strategies.

Author: Rita L Goad, PhD

- Entered network marketing industry in 1994.

- Married 40+ years.

- Mother of four.

- Built into the upper ranks with three different companies.

- Elite level, in top 1% of her current company.

- Her team includes over 1,300 distributors and 8,000 customers spread across seven different countries, and growing.

- Her team produces over one quarter of a million dollars in sales monthly.

- Has earned multiple incentive trips to fun destinations such as the Bahamas, Puerto Vallarta, and Cancun.

- In 2019, earned a $25,000 bonus by maintaining her elite rank for twelve concurrent months.

"The blessings are in the follow-up!!
And they flow both directions!"

- Rita L Goad, PhD

Rob's Notes: Rita is the master at following up. She practices what she teaches. Too many distributors don't have success because they won't master the boring necessary tasks to do so. I was approached by reps of 11 different network marketing companies before I joined my first one. Out of the previous 11, there were 3 that I was ready to join, but the person who contacted me never followed-up. They lost out on a massive income simply because they didn't follow-up.

Network marketing and farm life have something in common: They both require a lot of hard work! I grew up on a farm and learned to have an entrepreneurial spirit from my dad. He loved being his own boss and living his dream life on the farm, and he was willing to work hard to make that happen.

When I started network marketing, like most people, I was intrigued by the business model, but I didn't know exactly what I was getting myself into. This is a real business that takes hard work. Unfortunately, many people aren't willing to see it that way, or to do what it takes to build significant income. They are hopeful that it won't actually require work. Me too! Ha! I always thought it would be great to be paid to be a bum, but that isn't reality. That is not how success in anything happens.

I learned another important skill working alongside my dad on the farm: Follow-up! Follow-up is key to success! Farm work is never done. You never get to simply check a task off the list and move on. We were constantly following up on the farm. The animals all need follow-up, the chores need constant follow-up, the fields need follow-up... season after season... year after year.

Whether you are working on a farm or building a network marketing business, follow-up is vital. When I started network marketing, I had heard the phrase, "The fortune is in the follow-up." To me, this doesn`t fully paint the vision, because that phrase focuses only on me.

The complete picture of success goes beyond focusing on me. We benefit most by recognizing follow-up as the way we bless prospects` lives. I like to say, "The blessings are in the follow-up!" I often remind my team about this. When I don`t follow up with my prospect, I keep them from having the blessings they could have with the product or the business.

Consistency Is Key

Currently, experts say it takes an average of twenty-one touches or exposures for someone to get a "yes" to their offer in network marketing. That is a LOT of follow-up! You do have to be a source of information for your prospects in follow-up conversations, but it goes beyond this. Ask yourself, "Why would this person want to talk to me instead of going to Google or YouTube to get their questions answered?"

This doesn't mean that you have to talk to your prospects twenty-one times about the tool or product. Rather, it means multiple touches through personal conversation, which also will include tools and resource sharing. Consider all follow-up as relationship-building conversation. Show sincere interest in the person, and in what they are doing and going through in their life right now. Weave the blessings you have to offer into life conversations naturally and intentionally.

Don't ignore the fact that you need to talk about the business. But, don't mention it every time. You want people to be happy to see you. Do stay in front of your prospect with your follow-up one way or another.

I have a couple of key phrases I use to help take the pressure off of the prospect and help me not feel pushy. If I haven't heard from someone in a couple days after sharing the product or business info, I say, "I don't want to push, but I also don't want to leave you hanging. I just wanted to check back in and see if I can get you any additional information."

Another favorite phrase I use if it seems the prospect is avoiding a conversation is this, "If this isn`t a fit for you, no worries at all!" This often helps ease any pressure the prospect is feeling and keeps the door open for continued conversation.

Getting people interested in this business takes time. It is rare that someone wants to jump right in. People are all so busy, and this business and product are never as important for the prospect as it is for me or you. You and I are the ones that have to make follow-up a priority.

Be focused on the activity of following up, and don`t get hung up on the results. If you do the activity enough, the results will follow. Consistency matters, and follow-up is all about consistency. If you can stay consistent, it puts you FAR above the pack. Very few people will be consistent with their follow-up. Be one of the few!

Sometimes it takes months, even after the customer or prospect has said they want it. You have to be willing to focus on the activity and continue to commit to the process. Never think that following up gets to be checked off the list. Never stop the conversation!

Rob's Notes: Reread this sentence, because it is pure gold. "Sometimes it takes months, even after they have said they want it." You are playing the long game! This is a process. Some say yes right away. Some take a few weeks, and some take much longer. The follow-up process isn`t done even if they say no. Huge tip here. If one says no, then ask that person this. "It sounds like right now isn`t a great time for you. Are you ok if I keep you posted on everything?" This gives you permission to follow up later. Now don`t misinterpret what I am saying. Don`t pitch this person the next week. Instead set 2 reminders in your phone to reach out non-business related. One reminder in a few weeks and another reminder in a few months. No one likes the network marketer who approaches them every year about their products or business without any conversations in between. They perceive that network marketer as a TAKER. There is no set time when you should approach this person again as there are many variables. It could be four months later because you are just checking in. It could be sooner because you had a new product launch that you think would interest them from a customer or even business builder standpoint. The main point is be a good human being and remember that the follow-up never ends!

Follow-Up Will Build Relationships

Follow-up is a relationship building skill. There are several key relationships that you want to follow up with: Your community (local and social media), your prospects, your customers, and your team.

It is all about making connections and staying in front of people. Think about how you can connect and follow-up with people in your local or social media community. Are you being a blessing and really supporting people in the community? Are you being intentional with your time in the community? People may not be in enough pain right now for the product or the opportunity to be a great fit. But, when they are, I want to be the one they think of for a solution and someone that is interested in helping them. This is the real reason for the follow-up. We want to be a blessing in people's lives! If I am not consistent in connections and follow-up, then they may think of someone else when it is the right time.

I love social media. I have built my current business almost exclusively through social media. Three years ago, I had no clue how to do that. I just jumped in and began learning! You can do the same and start to utilize more of the tools you have available to follow up with your prospects and customers.

Messenger has made it so easy to connect to people without having their phone number. Using this, we can text, call, or send video and audio messages. It has been such a huge time saver. I remember homeschooling my kids by day and leaving my house at night to build my business the first time I did network marketing. I see social media as such a blessing because now I don't even have to leave my house as I build a business. It is such a joy knowing several moms on my team have been able to come home and build their business from home while being with their children! Be willing to step out of your comfort zone if necessary to learn the current tools and use them.

It can be scary or intimidating for some folks to learn something new. When I learned about social media, I watched other people and started listening to training about how to use it. But even when I jumped in, I really didn't know what I was doing. I just kept thinking that if they can do it, I can do it. Now, follow-up is more convenient and less time consuming than ever before!

Have a willingness to jump in and make 'mistakes`. This is literally the only way to learn and build new skills! You must be willing to fail in order to grow and succeed!

Social media is a huge blessing, but often people forget that you MUST follow up on social media. People misunderstand social media. It can be so helpful in building relationships, and the skills are basically the same as if you were sitting together in a coffee shop! Communicate regularly. Be a friend. Massively utilize written text, voicemail, or video to stay in touch and be a good, thoughtful human.

Few people get positive uplifting things from someone. I will send a quick message to people and tell them good morning, or tell them I am praying for them today. I simply send a quick positive message and they often send back a huge message telling me about what is going on with them. People are craving connection. I want to emphasize to people that social media is all about building relationships and being a blessing.

You also have to follow up with your team. This is non-negotiable. Reach out to your team. If you have a large team, reach out to maybe ten a day. Do it intentionally and purposefully, on a schedule.

This is a key skill of a leader. If you have one partner or one customer on your team, you are a leader. Start to follow up with the relationship and commit to continuing to follow up with them as your team grows.

Follow-Up with Your Own Training

One of the blessings I am most grateful for is the personal growth training I have experienced in network marketing. I don`t know who I would be today without it, but I do know who I am because of it. Even if I hadn`t made any money, the personal growth alone is worth the money and time I have spent. Personal growth takes truthful follow-up with yourself. You must hold yourself accountable. No one is going to check in with you to see if you are doing your own work.

You just have to do it. Take total responsibility for all of it. You have to listen to coaches and trainers, and then you have to do the work. It goes back to what I talked about earlier. You must be consistent. I can go train a whole group of people, but it isn`t the training that is important. It is what the individual is willing to do with the training that matters. It matters how they follow up with themselves.

I would love for it to just all work for everyone. But, the reality is, you have to be willing to do the work yourself, for the long-haul. That is what is going to make anyone successful, including you. We can all do better. We all have room for growth.

This industry has so much potential for the long-term. We need to help paint the picture for people and start to see the business for what it actually is. People are looking for a short-term huge success. It can happen, but for most, it doesn`t happen quickly. Start with no less than a 5-year plan and commitment. Be willing to be the example of hard work and dedication to your follow-up system and you will find success in the long-term.

Rob's Notes: That`s leadership. Lead by example. Follow up. Don`t be weak and give false hope. As a leader, emerging leader, or future leader, you must cast a vision that this is a real business. This is not a quick-fix overnight type of business. There are huge benefits to those that treat this like a real business and match their work ethic to their dreams.

Follow-Up Never Stops

I have always seen follow-up in network marketing as a lot like being a mom. There is never a "DONE" button. I am a blessed mom of four grown children. Just because my kids are adults doesn`t mean I stop being their mom. While the relationships do evolve, having adult children doesn`t mean I no longer have follow-up conversations with them. The relationships continue, conversations continue, and blessings continue. It is the same with the follow-up in network marketing. The follow-up never stops. It is simply a matter of 'what is the next conversation`?

Just because you got a sale or brought someone into the business doesn`t mean that follow-up stops. There is the follow-up before the sale and the follow-up after the sale. It doesn`t matter what your product or service is, continuing follow-up is a must!

Follow-up is about building relationships and continuing the conversations. The blessings are in the follow-up. Friendships are built in the follow-up. Lives change in the follow-up. No matter what, follow up, because that is how you will bless and be blessed.

There are endless follow-up systems and schedules. Just like parenting, you have to find what works for you and your team. You have to be willing to try new things and adjust. The main key is that you must be willing to invest in showing up and doing what you can to bless the lives of others.

Follow up! Because... The blessings are in the follow-up, and they flow both directions!

Author: Tina Joy Caroll

- In the four years, Tina has personally brought in over 1600 customers and affiliates combined. produced.

- Over four million dollars in sales last year.

- Ranked number 14 in the company.

- Over 10,000 affiliates on her team.

- Won six paid trips, spoke at nine company events.

- International speaker, who has shared the stage with Rob, Les Brown, Bob Proctor, Todd Falcone and Frazer Brookes.

"The way to get started is to quit talking and begin doing."

- Walt Disney

I started my network marketing venture by being prospected by the same person for almost two years. I always told them directly, "no!" and they kept asking why. To be quite candid, I thought network marketing was a joke and said all of the same things the haters would say. I saw it as a pyramid scheme with the idea that people at the top would be the only ones to make the money. I didn`t think anyone would take me seriously because of my past. One afternoon I got sick of corporate America and told my recruiter to break down the business. She invited me to the home of two inspiring leaders. At the conclusion of the meeting I told myself, if these people are accomplishing major goals then so can I. However, the exact opposite happened. I failed miserably for 13 months and lost money my first year between doing events and everything else. I didn`t give up hope, though. I knew my success would take time.

One night, I won tickets to a network marketing event in Las Vegas. This was the last dance. I was going to go all in and if it didn`t work out, I was going to go back to the corporate word. During the event, they asked anyone who was making six figures to stand up. All these women around me stood up. It was a lightbulb moment for me. I was like, "Ok, this works." It must be a "Tina problem" and not a "networking marketing problem." I had to figure out what they were doing and paid close attention to them. Behold it, the following month, I made four thousand dollars. It was an incredible month and one I would never forget. The team finally had a system in place, and we were all winning. I want to help you find your next rock star team member because they`re out there. The person you are afraid to reach out to could be the person who not only changes your life, but it could also change theirs.

After a lot of trial and error, I came up with my own plan. I knew what I had to do and how abundant the power of social media was on network marketing. I dove into the trenches and learned! Rob Sperry,

Frazer Brooks and Brian Fryer showed me how this would all work. Everything started to make sense and these three steps show you how simple it is to grow a network marketing business online.

Rob's Notes: Don`t ever underestimate the power of events! Tina is a perfect example of someone who`s now a six-figure earner on the verge of quitting. Events are like concerts. You can do your best to describe the feeling of how amazing the concert is, but your words will never do it justice. You just need to be there to see it for yourself, and at some point, take responsibility. The moment you stop blaming everyone else is when you focus on making your business stretch and multiply! I`ve coached Tina for years and had the great privilege of watching her grow as a leader.

Three Transformative Steps

The first step of transformation is finding who you are. Who are you, anyway? Many of us, especially women, can`t identify who we are since we allow our roles as wives or mothers to define us. Take this opportunity to identify three to five characteristics about you. My first thought was I love Disney. One day, I put my Minnie Mouse ears on and went live on Facebook wearing them. I wanted to stand out and I loved Disney, already had the ears, so gave it a shot. I had no idea I was creating a brand. That decision changed my life and branded me the hashtag, #TheSocialMouse. Truly ask yourself, "Why is this my thing?" Keep asking why until you can`t anymore. In fact, when I kept asking myself why Disney was my thing, I discovered I wanted to help people experience the magic of Disney and see the castle at Disney`s Magic Kingdom for the first time. I truly believe in the magic of Disney and wanted to share that with as many people as possible.

Again, look for three to five things that interest you. It doesn`t have to be anything flashy or unique! It`s important to be real and be who you are. We as women judge ourselves and others too much. We find ourselves indulging in our looks and outfits. Just be real.

To tell you the truth, I`m a recovering alcoholic and share this openly with others. At first, I used to be ashamed of it, but as I opened up with my past, it has connected me to some amazing people. Be willing to share your struggles with others. Your story gives people hope, and hope is the only thing stronger than fear. This also forced me to look at my mindset. In my past, I was not in the right place and over time slowly started to change it for the better. In fact, I started to have the same approach with my business, taking it one day at a time while working on my new daily habits. In other words, if you`re not feeding your brain good material to digest, then it will mentally crumble.

Have your mind squared, ready to go, and on hard days, have a good attitude prior to getting to work.

The second step is to find your people. Some people don`t know where to look. Facebook alone has three billion people. Consider starting there! After you have done step one, then you can identify with people that have similar interests. For me, Facebook groups have been impactful on my business! Compare it to the groups and clubs you were in in high school. If you were in the chess club, you would go and hang out with the chess club students. It`s the same concept with Facebook groups. Find the groups you can be a part of and participate with ease. Facebook groups have allowed me to turn strangers into friends.

Inside these groups we all share information. We have fun, and we get to know each other. The communication is easy to understand, and everyone knows where to look. If you`re having a difficult time finding common like groups, go back to step one. When ready, go to step two.

One of my friends used these transformation steps very well. She built her entire team around a Facebook group for "curly haired girls." An entire team!

Live streams are also very beneficial to the growth of your business and finding your people. People see your facial expressions, hear your voice and get to know you. The connection is much more meaningful and deeper than it is on a social media post. I use live stream to this day, and it is a huge part of my business.

Now let`s discuss your personal profile on social media. It`s like your living room, and you are inviting people to come to your house. What will be their first impression of you? Will they see a warm inviting space, or will they see a super spammy sales page? You want people to come to your profile and feel at home. This means letting them get to know YOU. Not your company or your product. Your profile picture should be of you. You should be smiling. Your cover photo should be a glimpse into your life. Maybe a family photo or a travel picture. It should not have anything to do with your company. Give people a reason to want to come and hang out on your personal profile. I can assure you that no one woke up today and thought to themselves, "Man, I hope I meet some super spammy person trying to sell me a product today."

Altogether, I`m very good at watching the trends in this business. I watch people get recruited into a company. They are so excited and on fire for 30, 60, or 90 days and then fall off the face of the planet. It dawned me that if I lasted longer than those people then I could become successful. That`s what I did. I stopped paying attention to the number of likes, comments, and followers that I generated. I focused on activities that produced results and results came! But it took time. In fact, many network marketers don`t give this business enough time to invest and quit. At first, I made a commitment that I would go live for 30 days straight. That turned into 90 days which in turn turned into 187 days. Between the 60 and 90 day mark, I experienced a tipping point. People started to notice my business and sent me messages. I went from being the hunter to being the hunted (in a good way)!

The third step is to be bold. Several years ago, I was a very broke single mother. I was making $9.75 an hour as a part time employee at Lowes mixing paint with no state benefits. Somehow, by the grace of God, I made it through that rough time in my life. I didn`t stick out to anyone, not one person came, prospected or told me about network marketing. At the time no one gave me the opportunity to change my life. I had no idea this amazing thing called Network Marketing existed. Had someone been bold enough to tell me about it, not only would it have changed my life, but it would have changed theirs. I turned out to be pretty dang good at it.

Who is missing out on the blessing of this industry because you haven`t told them about it yet? Your only job is to offer your prospects an opportunity. You never know who`s in desperate need of a financial change and who your next rock star recruiter will be. Don`t prejudge people. The broke struggling mother or the six-figure earner in the corporate world. You have no idea who will say yes unless you ask. Be bold and ask questions. Quite often we get caught up in our fears about reaching out to people and we forget just how badly someone is praying for the very thing you have to offer. In this business, take "you" out of the equation and ask yourself this question, "Are you willing to take a look at an opportunity that could change your life?" Now that`s a bold question.

Collect decisions from people. Ask them "Hey, is now a good time for you to get started?" It`s either a "yes" or "no." If they ignore me, that`s ok, but I took action in reaching out. I don`t get hung up on the answer. Not everyone replies with a "yes." I`ve gotten over 1600 customers and recruits in four years by keeping it simple and asking that one question. Want to get more yeses? One of the ways to get a "yes" is to be bold enough to share your story. Your real story. The one you think people will judge you for. More people are like you than you think, and when someone can connect to your story, they are more likely to want to join you in business or become your customer. I get it. I was so scared to be bold enough to share the hard parts of my story. I`m a high school dropout, teenage mother, and a recovering alcoholic. Most people didn`t believe I would amount to or accomplish anything. My story gives people hope and so will yours.

Whether inspiring or not, people love and want to follow a unique story. Stories provide leverage. Prospects want that mentor who`s been through the ups and downs. It`s common for people to be frightened about sharing their real story with anyone. Sharing can create shame and regret. However, more people share their stories than you think.

The more you share your story the more comfortable it is for others in the group to share theirs. Now I understand the impact sharing has on others. My inbox is always full! They tell me, "That is me. I thought I was alone." It means so much when we can all share our story.

Let me share with you a story. I saw the potential in one recruit. It was with this lady I saw on Facebook. She was a complete stranger. I knew she could crush it if I could get her to join the business. I kept thinking to myself, "If I could just recruit her, she would be amazing." I started by paying attention to her. During this time, there was a hurricane heading towards southern Florida where she lived, and she was getting prepared while taking care of a new baby. I didn`t know at the time what her husband did for a living, but it was clear he wasn`t going to make it home in time for the hurricane to hit land. I sent her a message. I let her know I was praying for her and her baby. I am sure she thought "Who is this lady praying for me?" but I reached out and I was genuine. It wasn`t long after that I got a message from her asking me about what I did. I shared the opportunity with her and within a few weeks she joined my team. To this day she`s one of my top leaders. You see, these steps work! I later asked her what made her say "yes." She told me because I was kind and genuine, and she watched my Facebook live streams when I wore my Minnie Mouse ears and shared the value of this amazing profession. Her husband would also ask her, "Who`s that lady with the Minnie Mouse ears, what are you watching?" Do you see how this whole story connects to the steps? Today, she`s one of my best friends. We have been to Vegas four times, Walt Disney World four times, we have been to three other states together, and we have hosted three leadership retreats together. What if I hadn`t been bold enough to reach out? Not only would I not have an amazing recruit in my organization, but I wouldn`t have one of my best friends today.

To be clear, this business doesn`t happen overnight. It took me four years of intentional hard disciplined work. I showed up every day. No matter how I felt. No matter how many people told me no. No matter who believed it would work. My job was to make sure that everyone knew about this amazing opportunity. Be willing to look at yourself, change your habits, if necessary. Be honest about where you are in life and what you need to work on. Don`t let bad days turn into bad weeks, months, or years. Always be willing to keep learning the skills to get better and better at this profession. Keep in mind the domino effect, and let it work in your favor. Adjust when you need to and ask for help if you need it. I can`t tell you how many times I`ve gone to Rob and said, "I need your help friend." Understand that you have to do these steps with repetition. Consistent action produces results. If I can do this, and I am a teenage mom, a high school dropout, and a recovering alcoholic then you can do this business too. The magic formula for success is deep down inside you! You have all the tools you need. Be brave enough to get out and make it happen. Maybe you don`t believe in you, but I do. Ears to your success. #TheSocialMouse

Rob's Notes: Stand out! No, that doesn`t mean you need to be loud It means step outside your comfort zone! How many times do you need to hear it? If you`re like me, you need to hear it several hundred times. Stop worrying about what everyone else thinks. I can tell you, people will judge you no matter what, so just be you! You may think your so-called weaknesses or past is scary to talk about, but those mistakes are what make you human. Those mistakes are what connect you to the outside world. Have the courage to be vulnerable, not in a whiny negative way but in the form of an empowering positive light. I love Tina`s boldness in sharing her past. Her vulnerability empowers so many!

Author: Erika Dale

- Only had $226 in her bank account when she started network marketing.

- Today, team does 1.2 million dollars a year in sales volume.

- Runs two online businesses with her husband Jesse.

- Erika`s intentions are to help people find what they`re passionate about.

- Creates meaningful life designs for those who want to transform their vision into reality and share it with others.

"If you continue to compete with others, you become bitter. If you continue to compete with yourself, you become better."

- Anonymous

Back in 2015, I was working 50 hours a week to make ends meet. At the time, I couldn`t figure out how to start a network marketing business. I didn`t have that kind of time to sit in homes and go to meetings. That time was focused on going to work. One night, I decided I wanted to learn more about social media and how to maximize it in order to turn it into a side hustle. When I started, I thought, "This is a no brainer! It just makes so much sense." I didn`t realize how many people were out there on social media. Over the past four years, I`ve been able to enroll over 630 people into my business through social media alone.

In my opinion, most people think social media will make it easier to succeed in this industry, but that`s not always the case. Yes, you can build faster, get in front of more people, and receive more followers or likes but at the end of the day the basics stay the same. You have to build a relationship with your audience based on friendship while being a professional at the same time.

Rob's Notes: I`ve found that those who are busy tend to be more successful in network marketing than those who aren`t. Busy people know how to utilize their valuable time. Put another way, urgency is synonymous with wealth. With Erika, she`s laser focused on income-producing activities at the highest level. Go to www.sperrybonus.com to download our top eight income producing activities. These will open up your eyes. Also, make sure to read about Erika`s ways to maximize the use of social media.

Don't be a Vanilla

I teach people to not be vanilla. What I mean is if everyone agrees with you (on social media), you're probably not being authentic or transparent with your content. That you're not saying who you really are. This will only push people away. Other times you may seem controversial to others with your posts. These are some obstacles you'll face when creating teams in your network. Don't be unexciting!

In one case, I had a couple people tell me they unfollowed me while another wrote how negative I was on my Facebook wall. I felt dumbfounded but got over it in a couple seconds. This business isn't for everyone, people are entitled to say what they want. No hard feelings. Not everyone is going to like you, and that's ok. Always be confident and know you're not always the right mentor for everyone. Aside from some of these challenges, keep expanding, put yourself out there, and create more value for your prospects.

When I was working in the gym, my reach was limited. Only 300 to 600 people a month were available to talk too. It was mostly the same people working out, and I realized it wasn't a good place for me to expand my network. The audience was too small. On the contrary, Facebook alone has 2.2 billion users. Imagine how many people you could reach there! That's a staggering number of users. When I rebranded online in East Asia, I connected with a customer in Taiwan. That customer sprouted more affiliates, and now I have a huge market in Taiwan connected to one of my Facebook groups. One of the ways I make a good impression with a prospect is by maximizing their value. I create rapport and become someone they know. When you search me on social media, you'll quickly find out how transparent I am.

Rob's Notes: People will judge you for being too fat or too skinny. People will judge you for being too poor or too rich. The mother of all fears is the fear of judgement. Get over it! As Erika pointed out, get comfortable with yourself. Be confident!

Pick It, and Stick to It

Do yourself a favor, pick one platform and become the expert in it before you start dabbling in another. If you can`t master one, then find another. I`m consistent at posting at least once a day on Facebook. Facebook is my business card and tells my customers I`m always open for business. Be consistent on your platform of choice and unlock the door for others to access your online business.

For the most part, Facebook encourages you to go live and host watch parties. Sometimes you`ll get that notification. On my team, we host many watch parties and teach our members how to set up their own. You can show anyone the instructions manual as long as it`s available on your forum. Your members may not be confident using it yet, but they can learn how to share it with their audience. Decide what works for you. Keep in mind, every system you put in place is another system you want others to learn. If you haven`t mastered the platform, then don`t take on anymore until you get the first one right. In other words, you don`t want analysis paralysis. Find that one platform you feel confident with.

Principally speaking, some people enter my network marketing group with only five Facebook friends. They probably aren`t going to be a social influencer their first year and that`s fine! Over time they will reach that point. There`s no timetable for success as long as your members put in the quality work to understand your social media platforms.

Consistently Follow up

One of the crafts I teach my team is the "play team technique." For instance, if you see a team member's post, go like it or make a comment. The more likes and comments you make, the more visibility it's going to expose to your Facebook friends and groups. Keep in mind, Facebook allows you to see who can see your likes and comments by adjusting the necessary filters in the privacy settings. Adjust accordingly. To add on, algorithms and social media are always changing. Try not to allow yourself to get bogged down by that. These main platforms make sure their sites and apps are easy to use. The basics are still the same. Keep on posting, create videos, and connect with people on messenger. Without effort, there's no gain!

As several hours go by on my post, I wonder how many crickets are in the room. I wonder if the internet is broken! If you post and aren't getting many likes or comments, you can message your friends or followers to check it out. Ask them to like or make a comment. Do your best to get your content out there in front of your network. The more engaging you are with your audience (friends, followers, group pages, etc.), the more they'll respond back. A Facebook broadcast will usually do the trick. Be a student in the art of social media. New applications are introduced every hour on the app store. Do your due diligence and stay up to date on new software that may aid you in your business network.

On occasion, I've had several people in my downline ask what active promotions are currently available on my posts. These are great questions to ask if you're doing really well in your business. It comes to show those who ask questions are the ones who have better results in comparison to those who don't ask questions. In other words, do your best to share with your groups often. If you don`t, you`ll slowly lose your members as they`ll feel less motivated to work with you. I try to post more than once a day, but not more than thrice a day. Be flexible. Spread your posts at different times of the day. If I post all at once, then I wait 3 to 4 hours before the next post. Basically, if you post at 7:00 am and then an hour later at 8:00 am, people won`t see that 7:00 am post due to Facebook`s algorithms. The idea is people aren`t going to your timeline and scrolling. You need to let that post marinate to let your audience have a chance to like it and comment. The same Facebook algorithms apply to everyone using this platform. Make sure to post throughout the day.

I strongly recommend having a Facebook group page for your team and one for your prospects. At times, I`ll combine my customers and prospects together because it`s a great way to upscale and integrate your team. Eventually all prospects become members, but I believe a prospect group is necessary. It doesn`t have to be fancy and you don`t have to pay someone, you just have to start. Ask everyone to post on the group. Give them ideas to post about. Assign an administrator every two weeks and make that administrator pick a new one for the next two weeks when their time is up. This is a good way for everyone to feel integrated as a leader and will give them an opportunity to introduce new team members. Other times, I`ll put my customers and prospects together since my prospects sell to customers. Open the channel for your prospects.

Life Happens Outside of Social Media

By and large, you have to work on improving the quality of your content if you`re not seeing the results you want. Besides learning on social media, reading books, listening to podcasts, going to company events, being part of the community, do the masterminds or get a coach. When you`re learning, you are able to yield back the knowledge to your affiliates.

What I love about Facebook the most is you can bond quickly. People get to know you by what you write and post. If you aren`t writing stories yet, then start! Quite often I see posts written with "my." This context will say, "like my product" or "like my post." There`s no connection with people here and my husband struggled with this. He would get frustrated since he would go live, make a post, and not get any traction. I asked him if he was reaching out to his audience afterward, liking and commenting on their posts. He said no. He wasn`t scrolling on his feed to see what his friends were posting. The point is, you have to be intentional online and in person. Eventually I taught my husband to like and make comments on his audience`s news feed five minutes before he made a post or went live. By doing this, he was able to attract more people to his post or livestream, rather than one person to none. He saw the difference and thanked me by making my favorite food dish!

To get to the topic at hand, if you want to receive engagement, you must first be engaging. You wouldn`t go out with your friends for lunch to only talk about yourself all afternoon. The best approach is to ask them questions, be interested and contribute. This identical theory bears similarity to any other platform. Don`t be the person that`s all about you! Be interested. Live a life where you connect with others by sharing the same space, talking about each other, sharing your plans and showing your integrity.

Rob's Notes: Erika and her insights remind me why I initially didn't have success on social media. For five years I didn't post one thing that would help my business. I was fearful for doing it the wrong way. Finally, I woke up and committed to posting every day. When I did this, everything changed. Sure, I had some pretty awful Facebook posts at first. When the date came, they popped up as annual Facebook memory posts. Meanwhile, as I started to post daily, the quality of my posts improved. They became more authentic, engaging to watch, and my audience noticed my niche! To be honest, I only fabricate my posts in five categories. If there was something that didn't fall into one of those categories, then I wouldn't post it. The objective is about consistency. At first, you won't be great, but if you stay committed to posting daily on one platform, your audience will start to notice.

Author: Nicky Rempel

- Been in the industry for 7 years.

- Earned multiple 7 figures.

- Built teams in 5 countries.

- Spoken on many stages.

- Was an Ambassador of Network Marketing Hall of Fame in business for home magazine 2018.

- Awards in company for
  - Top duplication
  - Highest volume growth
  - Top in helping people get quick start bonuses.

- In 2018, was awarded a very prestigious award that one distributor receives a year for exemplifying certain characteristics that the company values.

- 2nd fastest million-dollar earner in the company.

- Tied as the fastest to one of our top ranks.

"If it is to be, it is up to me."

I was one of those leaders who was born at a conference. When I went down to Nashville, I met simple average, ordinary people who were making extraordinary incomes. On day two, this woman got up on stage and her speech inspired me. She was a full-time dental hygienist. As a mother, she was making more than the dentist through her network marketing business part-time. That was a defining moment in my life. How could someone make more than their boss part time while working for them full time? I told myself that the next time I came back to the conference, I`d be successful like them with an inspiring story to share.

Over time, I became one of the company`s fastest-growing members to reach executive level in 10 weeks making $10,000 a month. I started to become a mentor to so many, and affiliates started looking up to me! Building a team contributed to my success, but I credit the work I did on my personal development the most.

On my team, recruiting is our number one skill. If we aren`t recruiting, then we`re in management mode. Being a network marketer also requires facing rejection. Set the expectations for your business module. If you stop recruiting, your team will follow the same path, and your business will drop. We see this happening all the time in other businesses. Lead by example and your members will follow. To be honest, recruiting is the most vital skill to have and must be used correctly. Recruiting is finding a need and filling it for that person. Listen to your prospects` needs. A lot of times their answer is they want to make more money, and that`s fine. Creating meaningful relationships while working as a team to produce massive income is essential.

Recently, my company asked me to share my story on how I train my affiliates in recruiting. I was doing incredible things in a short duration of time for my team, and they wanted to know how I was doing that.

I told them the truth. Recruit and follow up! I explained how the business structure worked. A lot of prospects and customers were drawn in by the warm welcoming culture my group brought. People loved that and wanted to join or refer business to me. Have a good recruiting pitch. It only takes little to grab someone`s attention with a simple quote that`s powerful enough to engage them. That one person may turn into two and multiply into many more.

Rob's Notes: I had the privilege of coaching Nicky the last few years. If something doesn`t work for her, she moves on. As I mentioned earlier, this shows we all have different personalities and styles of learning. To tell you the truth, Nicky doesn`t major in minor things! However, she implements the most important part in network marketing. She opens her mouth and recruits. She lives by the mantra "The speed of the leader, the speed of the pack."

Recruiting Influencers

My most favorite part about recruiting is finding influencers. I like to find out where they hang out. I always pick them out in the room. They're the ones I spend time with the most. I had to act like an influencer in order to attract the influencers.

Recruiting influencers is important for long-term success. They come in all forms. For instance, I recruited a girl four years ago who was well connected in the diet and health industry. When she saw my vision and joined my team, she recruited other like-minded influencers. She became one of my top leaders. I knew she could build a team by introducing this business to her clients.

When you look at different industries people thrive in, you see what kind of influence they have in their sector. They could be selling a product or a service already and sell even more to their clients. Before I started network marketing, I was building many relationships with people. When I asked them to join me, I had known most for quite some time. Some of them would say, "If Nicky is doing this, then I want to do it." The business didn't scare people off. They knew their friends joined and trusted me, which propelled them to join, as well. I tell my team this all the time: if people don't trust you, it'll make the recruiting process more difficult. Build trust first, then recruit.

For the most part, my approach with people is simple. It's direct and upfront. I don't beat around the bush. I'm forward in letting them know that I want to work with them. I tell my prospects what my team is looking for and how their expertise or skills can make a positive impact. People like it when I'm honest. I continually work on my people skills so eventually, it has become very natural. I have a really good friend that asks when I`m going to stop trying to recruit him. I always tell him, "Never, until you tell me to stop! I care about you too much to see this opportunity pass you by!"

It`s important to know how to read people. It`s something I`ve learned over time. The more I understand personal development, the more I`m able to understand my prospects. At first, this approach wasn`t innate with me. This type of engagement took me 10 years to master. These are skills anyone can learn. You have to be open and willing to learn them step by step. Know your audience and pay attention to who your recruiting.

One of my favorite parts about recruiting influencers is they know how to overcome adversity. They`re not skeptical and typically have enough money to buy whatever you`re selling. Influencers don`t put their name behind it until they know it`s legit and something their audience will love. A non-influencer doesn`t care. They only want to make money. You see the difference between the two? When you align top influencers with leaders, more knowledge is shared. This allows like-minded influencers to connect and share valuable ideas with each other. In turn this leads to increasing team members and sales. This also allows other networks to collaborate, share social media platforms, and integrate thousands of followers with provisional resources available to increase recruiting and follow up skills. Influencers get it, when they bring what they got to the table, other like-minded influencers will share and make your team grow faster than normal.

Recruiting the Influencer's Circle

Recruiting is all about connecting with people you know and don`t know. The ones that don`t know you have no reason to listen. Several people on my team are from different cities. I didn`t know them personally at first, but now they`re all huge influencers. I had to figure out how to recruit without overwhelming them.

Before I engage with the contact, I`ll see if they`re on Facebook. I want to see their comments, their posts, what mutual friends we share, read their about section and look at their photos. This provides me feedback before introducing myself. "Hi, it`s nice to meet you, I see you also know John Smith and Mary Betty, two good friends of mine whom I`ve known for years. I actually met them in Los Angeles at this amazing jazz and blues party on the Sunset Strip. Anyway, may I ask how you know John and Mary, as well?" I opened up the conversation by sharing what mutual friends we had. They got excited and then talked about what industries we worked in and how network marketing plays a huge role.

About a month ago, I recruited three big influencers who are now on my team. To be quite candid, I`m not heavily connected to many big influencers. But I knew, by reaching out to them with mutual friends, they would be more interested in doing what I do. What big influencers wouldn`t want to make more money? If we didn`t have mutual friends, I would use another strategy to connect. Now these influencers are coming to my house with new prospects to sign up. Talk about simple steps with noteworthy outcomes!

Influencers don`t always seem who they appear to be. I wouldn`t have considered myself an influencer, either. But now when you ask my team, they say I`m one of the greatest influencers in the industry. In order to be an influencer, you have to be a leader. See how others thrive in different industries. People have this idea that it`s the wealthy and most prominent individuals who are the leaders. On my team I have a list of influencers with their biographies. Not all started from wealthy backgrounds. In addition, you also want to have influencers with multiple circles. Now I think about all the people whom I`ve known the past five years that see me in this position. I wanted them to see me as their leader in order to attract other like-minded individuals.

When finding success in this industry, you have to have the right mindset. I didn`t have this before, but now I carry myself with a powerful mindset to inspire others. I`m grateful for all my affiliate members and give Rob credit for giving me the tools to become a leader of influence. To be honest, if we aren`t a person of influence or believed to be, we won`t attract those prospects. First impression counts. You want your audience to see the picture you create.

One of my good friends is connected to a well-known influential person in this industry. She`s not necessarily someone I think would do great in this business but saw what kind of potential there was. Long story short, she became an incredible leader due to the influence she had in her network. She had many friends who trusted her very well that gave them reason to join her business. This shows the power of changing your mindset when you create the vision you want your audience to see.

The Simple Strategy

There is a simple strategy that I teach my entire team. If your market is cold (meaning they don`t know you personally), then you have to build trust before you sign up your prospects. Start by saying, "Hey, if I were able to show you how you could create your own economy, would you watch a couple of videos?" If they reply "yes," then I reply, "Does it work for me to call you back tomorrow night? Does that give you enough time to watch 20 minutes worth of videos?" Before you send any videos, get the follow-up appointment. That`s the most crucial part. Once they give confirmation, send them the videos and tell them how excited you are to chat with them tomorrow.

When I do my follow-up, I have a three-way call. The third person would be someone in my upline or an influencer. They`re there to strengthen the potential bond more with this prospect. "I texted my mentor, and they have some time to share their story with you before we talk, so I`m going to add them to the call." When I add a third party to the call, I identify all parties and get the conversation rolling away! Toward the end, my mentor closes by saying, "Nicky is going to send you this link to get you started." You see, instead of me saying it, my influencer says it, and they hop off the call. You see how this recruitment strategy works? It`s really that simple.

The prospect is impressed and nurtured. They feel no pressure while we share information about our company. That`s why this system is so great. All we do is say simple words and phrases, get prospects on the phone, trade-off who will be providing information, and who`s speaking next. This is real planning and we teach this strategy to our team. They think they`re on the phone with a rock star and will feel encouraged to say "yes" or eventually do so. Doesn`t matter if you are brand new in the industry or a seasoned leader, we stick to the plan because it`s simple and it works.

Also, there is a simple onboarding system that we send at that moment of sign up that helps them get connected quickly and a step by step guide to ensure their success as well.

Rob's Notes: Leonardo Da Vinci once said, "Simplicity is the ultimate sophistication." You`ll hear over again how leaders like Nicky talk about keeping it simple and taking action with income producing activities. Let`s say you`re currently reaching out to three new people daily. That`s over 1,000 contacts made over the course of the year. Now add third party validation with 20% of those contacts. The third-party validator is the person in your upline or an influencer. Practicing these methods will improve the nature of your invite, follow-up, and closing speech. You`ll get better at handling objections while gaining more confidence. In today`s industry, we see too many network marketers perplexing their plan. They fail to remember reaching out to new people. The business model is not only easy to understand, but it`s simple to duplicate. Do what you have to do and set your expectations to earn the results you want.

A u t h o r : R e e s e   P i e r c e

- 6 years in industry.

- Sold over $1,032,039 in products.

- In under two years she reached the top two percent in the company.

- Rank of 100k.

- In the last 23 months, originated 734 team members from US, Canada, and UK.

"I am not what happened to me,
I am what I choose to become"

- Carl Gustav Jung

One of my favorite facts about network marketing is the ability to break the imaginary barrier we typically create. When I was 15 years old, I became a mother. During that time, I had many limiting beliefs about what I would be able to accomplish when I conceived children. I never thought I would overcome my sense of shame or find other women and men who could relate or be inspired by my story. It`s an incredible feeling to read messages from people who have heard my story and use it as a catalyst to break their own life barriers.

Attraction marketing is using social media and other online platforms to build an audience. I`ll share some simple steps you can use to grow your network marketing business. You`ll get to see how creating authentic content will attract and engage your audience more than ever. This helped me become the six-figure earner I wanted to be. Attraction marketing is an ongoing commitment to support people as they get to know you and analyze your authenticity. In other words, brand yourself first before introducing any kind of product.

Be Authentic

Authenticity is the backbone of a solid network marketing business. Naturally, people want to connect with others, and as professionals, there`s only one way to market. From 2011 to 2018, I lacked the expertise in attraction marketing. I wasn`t showing people who I really was. My business changed when I started to share my life experiences with others. Learning strategies to connect and grow my engagement took time to learn. I can think of one great example; one time I posted a picture on my Facebook page. It was a picture of the mess in my house. I wrote,"a messy home is one of the things that make me the crankiest! I am so relieved I found these products to keep me sane throughout this day." This post attracted the attention of many mothers who were looking for the same sense of relief. There was a huge influx of people that commented on my post. They felt my distress. Moreover, these mothers wanted to connect since they saw how "real" of a mother I was and could trust me. This allowed me to connect with them more to talk about my product.

Do your best to be authentic. Attraction marketing has brought me success while allowing me to share parts of my life with others. When you strip down, get raw and real with people, it can bring you much success.

Speak to the One

Your audience wants to know you. They follow you because they see something in you they like. Over time, they`ll build trust with your posts as they see them more. Real authenticity is exposed here. The conversations can be thrilling. In fact, think of one person that would like to hear from you right now or from your next post. People do not care about the product or the opportunity. They care about seeing a better version of themselves when they engage with your posts. Show them your struggle and share your story. For many years, I`ve battled anxiety and depression. My audience listens to my story and some relate back. My goal is to make a connection with those like-minded individuals.

While "masses" of people may be reading your content, your goal is to talk to that individual one on one. It`s about relating to that one person and bringing them on a journey. Take them with you on your boat instead of watching them from the sideline. Let them see the horizon and your vision. If you do this correctly, people are going to find themselves attached to all your stories. That`s exactly what you want with your clients, prospects, affiliates members, or customers. Over time, they`ll develop into leaders themselves. It`s all about how you deliver your crafted post. Who cares if it impacts thousands of people because it isn`t about how many likes you get; it`s about creating value in several individuals with whom you can connect.

Rob's Notes: Reese said something you need to read again. "Who cares if it impacts the masses. It isn`t about how many likes you get." This hits home for me big time! I wish I could have had that attitude sooner in my career. In fact, I mention this in my book *The Game of Conquering* and on my website, [www.thegameofconquering.com](www.thegameofconquering.com). To be honest, I didn`t post anything on social media for five years despite being the number one recruiter out of a million distributors. I was scared of what others thought of me. One day I got over myself and shared my stories on social media. In my first year of Facebook live streaming, I averaged about 10 comments per live video. As a full time coach, my training spanned across 40 nations but yet only received an average of 10 comments per live stream. It felt deflating but I kept my consistency going. After a year, I got better at utilizing the live steam platform on Facebook. This was when my comments and page likes sprouted in staggering numbers. I was receiving 100 comments per live video. When you focus on the progress and not the outcome, the results will follow.

Tell Your Story

The concept behind attraction marketing is that it brings stories back to our lives. Stories sell and people connect to them. Be prompt and truthful in crafting your story. Telling a story is more impactful than saying, "Hey, I just joined a company, you should join my team." Even better, explain why you joined the company, what got you to that point.

In my story, I had many years of failure, rejection, and fear. I was paralyzed not knowing what to do and questioning myself. Someone that really helped me overcome this is Ray Higdon. I knew I would always start my success journey when the time was right.

Human connection isn't about the sale, it's about being able to see people and be seen back equally. Be authentic and trustworthy. We can start by telling what happened in our story, and how it led us to expand our business. When we practice attraction marketing, we keep the fire burning always; we're always working. You don't want to become this laser-focused salesperson that's always pushing a product or a business opportunity. Also, when talking in your living room doing a Facebook livestream, make sure you show your audience that you're an ordinary human being who breathes the same air.

For the most part, the last approach you want to have is selling your product first. It should start with your own voice and why. Brand yourself first. How did your life change? Commonly, everyone has something to share. People get stuck thinking they don't have a story to post since they don't write well enough to share. Take a second to reflect and think why you started using this product, how did you find it, how did it make you feel beforehand, what happened when you used it and how did it change your day-to-day routine? When asking yourself these questions, you`ll realize you do have a story to tell. That`s the reason why you got involved in this business.

Here are a couple tips to help you get started with attraction marketing. First, find five people that you can relate to and ask yourself why. Why did this person make me feel this way? Second, why did you share their post or reference their podcast? Third, did it make you think, laugh, or connect you to the intended recipient? Last, ask yourself what you learned? Write down ways you related to the piece you posted about.

At times we`ll share astute striking posts since it resonates with us. What that means is the content is impactful enough to share with our followers. By doing this, we show our influence, since the audience is now relating to our post through desired interest. This creates mutual bonding. In other words, we want to evaluate our online presence by looking at data that gives us an understanding of the types of people who engaged with our posts, such as Facebook Analytics.

In the morning, I always listen to podcasts. I recently heard one that made me think about different topics. In order for me to share it, I had to reference the podcast a specific way by providing takeaways to my followers. It transitioned from being "copy and paste" to a very engaging post that captured the attention of my followers. The more drawing your content is, the more satisfied your viewers will be. This is a huge deal since they`ll start to see your content as a reliable source of information.

Rob's Notes: In all due process, attraction marketing is not about making a post praying the masses will join. After reading this phenomenal chapter by Reese, I hope you have a much better understanding on what this type of network marketing entails.

The author gave one of the most in-depth training segments about "attraction marketing." Your goal is to increase your visibility, connect with more people, stand out, and attract those who resonate your style. In reality, the goal is not to be everything to everyone. If you try to do this, you will be nothing to no one! To make it simple, your goal is to build the trust bridge authentically. It's true you'll need to reach out to new prospects on a consistent basis. When you follow the formula Reese recommended, you'll have more success in reaching out to potential prospects or a next born leader.

Author: Taylor Kirby

- Single dad.

- 6 figure earner.

- Entrepreneur, influencer, and speaker.

- Experience in both the corporate and affiliate side of the industry.

- Built team of elite leaders with over 370,000 affiliates.

- One of the highest ranks in his company.

"Men don't follow titles, they follow courage. If you would just lead them to freedom, they'd follow you."

- William Wallace (Braveheart)

My network marketing campaign started after I graduated from university. I joined the company when it launched in 2002. At the time, I knew the company founders very well. They asked me to join, which I did, but not on the networking marketing side. I joined the corporate side. For my first six years, I saw the company go from zero dollars to making $600 million a year. The business showed me the possibilities distributors had. One of the founders of the company mentored me and I saw how fiercely protective he was of the brand. I learned many valuable lessons from him which provided benefit over the course of my career. As a young single guy in my twenties, I was able to travel the world and met amazing leaders. These leaders are still some of my mentors and good friends to this day.

Sometime later, I got recruited by another company that was fairly new. This opportunity allowed me to meet more emerging leaders who showed me another way to build, train, teach, and grow a team business. My new company taught me the power to connect, gain reputation and seek out social influence.

Many of the executive team members were very well integrated while using their connections to quickly gain leaders, funding and influence. I was there when the company imploded and saw first-hand what power and greed did to corporate staff and distributors. It went from success, re-building success, to failure - all in that sequence.

To be quite candid, I learned more throughout these years than many other distributors would have. I met some of the most talented corporate members in the industry and many distributors who have gone to become outstanding leaders. I saw the effort they put into training and mentoring their teams. They utilized their compensation plans to get the most out of their efforts. It wasn`t until the next company I joined that I switched sides from secretary to becoming a distributor.

Globally, I have seen it all. The corruption, power, and greed. In addition, I`ve seen the drive to succeed, the compassion, and service. All sides of the industry do exist. It`s a matter on how you make the right connections with people.

The recruitment process is always different between companies. I love when people say they don`t have what it takes to succeed in this business, they weren`t the first ones "in," or the company is too old. These are not excuses to limit your earning or leadership potential. Can you imagine if people decided to not shop at Target because it was too old?

Ten years have gone by, and now I have over 370,000 affiliates in my network. My recruiting strategies are accountable for my success. Regardless if you`re starting your journey now or been in the business for many years, the building blocks for success still stay the same. Keep learning to dial into your recruiting techniques and continue to build your network. Reach out to people from all backgrounds. People are motivated for different reasons to succeed. Have their work ethic in your group. If you want to continue growing your business, you must continue building your team, set an example, follow up, and recruit! The top earners always recruit.

Find the Plan, Solve the Problem

I`m a bearded single man making an amazing living selling to a market that`s 99% women. Over the years, I`ve learned to say, "How can I help you relieve a little bit of your stress?" That`s what`s it all about for me. People aren`t looking for leadership titles, they`re simply looking to ease the financial strains in their life. They`re looking for relief from those unexpected expenses that keep piling up.

> **Rob's Notes:** I`ve known Taylor for years. He lives 10 minutes from me. Besides hanging out at masterminds, we go to lunch every so often and catch up. If anyone could create an excuse not to lack success, he could. It`s assumed being in a company where it`s 99% women is perceived as nearly impossible for a male, but not for my man Taylor. In other words, stop making excuses and take massive action on your business.

I would like to acknowledge one of my good friends that lives in the beautiful state of Hawaii. He has labeled himself as the world`s laziest networker. He always says the art of recruiting comes down to what fits your goals and needs. Let your new prospects build up their network while you build up yours. Show them how it`s done first so you can let them go out and amplify. If we know when someone`s power drive is about to shut off, we`ll come to their aid to prevent that measure from happening. We all win when we all collaborate together on our marketing efforts.

You see, the person in front of you isn`t worried about hitting six figures and going to network events. They`re more concerned with how they`re going to pay their electric bill due next Friday. Don`t sit here and say that people can't make a million dollars in two years, or that it's far out of their reach. In other words, don't bring up their pain points or their struggles. These thoughts will hinder your team down if brought up. This will prohibit a positive mindset from developing in your group if you keep bringing up their stories. Let them share their stories if they have too. Last thing you want is your affiliates to walk away.

Learn to listen. Everyone talks about the power of social media and how it's a massive recruiting tool. I do not spam everyone I know or see. Want to know how I recruit on Facebook? I read people's posts. For example, there may be a post like "Oh man, my water heater just went out, this is not the time for this! This is the last thing I need right now!" "OMG, my car just got hit!!" In my observation I see people posting about their stress points, things they can't afford to buy, or worries about next month's rent bill. When I see a variety of different posts, I ask myself these questions, "Do I think this will work for them, are they truly hungry for success, and how am I going to approach their needs?"

Several months ago, I had a call with an amazing girl who was trying to make it in the music industry. She's in her early thirties, had to move back in with her parents, and I saw her pain mount. She also has a massive number of followers on her social media profile, which meant she was very engaged in her industry. In my mind, this presented a good opportunity for her to get involved in network marketing. I wanted to show her what she's capable of. I wanted her to see a vision of running a successful marketing business and being the music star she wanted to be. I knew she wanted to move out of her parent's home as soon as possible and could make it happen! To me recruiting has become way less hype and more about helping people obtain better livelihoods.

I want someone who's hungry, who's willing to put in the work and who has a "hot button." If you aren't looking for relief, then this industry won't work for you. When people see this as an opportunity to make extra money to pay for Christmas, to pay a down payment for a car, or pay for their children's expenses, then they see the big picture. Brace for impact and go all in! I've heard some pretty vivid stories in this industry. I heard one story about a member who was able to buy a new set of tires and pay for their broken HVAC unit in only one week of being in the business. These are prime examples of leaders and affiliates collaborating together.

I'm able to bring people onboard since I provide a solution to their pain points. I've been with the same company for over ten years and crossed many ambitious teams with well-trained, enlightened leaders. I studied how my actions, consistency, and daily presence became the driving force to my credibility. This has helped me continue my efforts in recruiting new people.

I love it when people don't lie about what amount they receive from their commission paycheck. Affiliates, recruits and prospects are always welcome to see what I earn, look at my team volume and see how expansive my business is on Excel data charts. There's nothing for me to hide, which is why people trust me. Let's go have some fun and I'll show you how to do it!

Rob's Notes: Over a year ago, I remember seeing Taylor jump on Facebook lives at 11pm, sometimes later at night. I thought he was absolutely crazy! I mean who would be on this late anyway? Months go by and I start seeing hundreds upon hundreds of viewers on his live streams. So why does this matter, and how does this tie in to everything? Taylor provides insane value and shows up daily to work. He's a top recruiter from his actions and shows up consistently for others. He understands their pain points, knows how to best serve them, and even his cold audience feel like they have a connection with him.

Your Biggest Recruiting Tool

Your biggest recruiter is your success. That`s the beauty of the company. When you hustle and grind, you`ll have success. When you bring someone on board who`s brand new, teach them to sell. Sell yourself to understanding the recruiting process. It doesn`t matter how you sell, but once you consistently do, your recruitment strategy will be easier to amplify making it easier to teach this vital skill.

Your excitement is what sells. Are you willing to use all your motivation and energy to run a business? I look at network marketing and tell people, get in and start selling. This is where your recruiting power transforms. Trainees want to know that you`re capable of leading. They don`t want to join knowing you can`t show them the ropes. They want this stress factor crossed off knowing you can show them the ways. In other words, give your trainees confirmation.

Dive in, go live and show people your success. I don`t care if it is $20 or $100, show people that you are taking massive action on your business module. In fact, let your followers know that you made $100 this week. Get them eager and thrilled! Be aware that people are always watching you. You never know who might be inspired by that $100 sale you made for them to sign up a dozen new associates the next day. Some people are still watching me ten years later.

One morning, someone reached out and said, "I`ve been watching you for several years; I`m finally interested in joining your company." I also have classmates who reach out from college. I`ve been blown away at how many people are always watching. People want to see my house, watch me on vacation and see me when I`m driving my car around. If I`m absolutely making money doing the things I want, they want to see that on livestream for themselves. Keep in mind, before people dip their toes in, they want to see that it`s possible for them to make money. Let people make their observations and wait until the timing is right for both you and the prospect to connect.

Honesty is the Best Policy

In network marketing, you have to be transparent with people. For example, if you lie about your business in the recruitment process, word of mouth goes out quickly, and you`ll be known as the bait and switch person. For your sake be honest; it`s very simple. Honesty and integrity are significant aspects to your credibility, reputation, and why someone would want to partner up with you.

You can`t recruit and not expect to answer questions about your accountability. When you answer their questions and concerns, it allows your prospects to grow faster and be more confident in you as their role model. Honesty is what you`re using to build your team and create your team`s culture. When you say "Here`s what I expect from you, here`s what you can expect of me," and you stick with it, they`ll learn to perform, adapt, and meet your expectations.

I don`t believe in "bait and switching" anyone for any reason. Eventually, your transparency will reveal. Make sure it comes out with good intentions to help others. Back in August, I bought this beautiful colorful tapestry for $200 on Instagram for my daughter. When it came in the mail, she was so excited to open it. When she opened it, it was the ugliest thing I`ve ever seen. It didn`t even look like the picture described. It was garbage. It was nasty yarn and was nowhere near the size advertised, it was tiny. This is "bait and switching." I was so angry and disappointed. When I called their customer service number to complain, the phone disconnected. That`s not how you do business. Don`t be that person in this industry. If you`re lying about what you make, how much real work it takes to succeed, or about your leadership rank, the person will eventually find out over time and they will be disappointed. Be honest. Tell them success takes time and to step out of their comfort zone. Sometimes you`ll fail; other times you`ll succeed, and you`ll sell and grow.

My recruit system is different. You never know who`s going to go and if or when you`ll have an issue with someone. You have to be open with everyone. This industry is more than a system. It`s diverse, dynamic, and very transparent. People are motivated for different reasons to succeed. Let your affiliates thrive their work ethic on your team. It`s a numbers game. You win some affiliates and others go; you have to keep networking. You`ll see the ones that want to work with you, but let them see their business in their own light. Let them talk to their own customers and use your business modules for guidance, if needed. Besides your team members, the customers are the pillar for your foundation.

Now that I look back at those who I thought would be rock stars, some did, and others dropped out. I still get a little bit shocked. Some walk the walk, and others talk the talk. There have been a few wild cards who I never expected would become some of my biggest leaders. Why? Besides their determination to work, they needed someone to believe and encourage them. Their fuel lit on fire, and that`s what they needed while taking their "pain point" and using it as motivation.

When my members get started in this business, I never pay them to get started. What I found interesting is if they don`t sacrifice initially, then what makes you think they`ll put in the work. They won`t develop any skin in the game and will lose without trying.

In all my years involved in this business, I remember there were a couple of people who I did help with the initial cost. For one of those, their kit was active for over six months untouched. Their box still had the tape seal unopened. As motivated one can be to excel in the business, when you pay for their materials, it`ll change their desire to succeed, since it won`t feel like it`s their financial independence of which they took 100% ownership. However, for the other person I helped, she was noticed.

I remember seeing her. She walked around the expo. She came up asking us how much the products were and how much commission she could make. Fifteen minutes later she came back with tears in her eyes and said, "I have $10 in my bank account. I can`t go grocery shopping and we have no food at our house. My husband and I both lost our job yesterday. Honestly, the only reason why we`re here is we were given these tickets. We decided to come check it out and eat free samples, because we`re hungry."

She told us how successful she could be in the business but didn`t have the initial cost to pay for the sign up-fee. She told me if we could help her out, she would pay us back in a week. She also proposed that if she was given a $100 worth of product, she would return to our booth with everything sold the next day. I couldn`t believe I was about to give someone $100 worth of product. I knew how desperate she was, and her story inspired me to help. The next morning when the expo opened, she was back and sold everything.

She paid me back the sign-up fee, the $100 worth of product and made her commission sales. She was such a rare case, so broke and yet made it work. I could have never seen this woman again, but she came back. Long story short, she went from surviving on her welfare check not being able to feed her family to making $40,000 a month in three years. The rare opportunity I gave her changed her life.

My members come from all diverse backgrounds, and one of the unique aspects about this business is that we all start out the same way. Some of the ladies on our team come from abuse, loss, or countless other life trials. When I meet them for the first time, their life is on downward auto pilot. They join because they`re depressed and want to be part of a team that cares. Other`s sign up from referrals or their friend`s ask them to join.

I`m all about supporting everyone. One of my affiliates, an outstanding high energetic woman, signed up seventy people her first month. Seventy is a lot! Then I found out she had a huge network of clients who used her professional hairstyling service to cut their hair. I remember when she made her first post on social media. She told everyone what new business she got into and her clients came on board. It`s stories like hers that touch my heart. Every day I continued to fuel my passion, drive, and desire to help other affiliates win!

The art of recruiting is key, but the real power is in the follow-up, and no, follow-up wouldn`t exist without recruiting. You have to make sure they`re opening up their own box. Have them do it on Facebook live, invite some friends over, it doesn`t matter what they do as long as you follow up. Be willing to answer all dynamic questions. These questions remind me when I started out as an affiliate. It`s good to know what it`s like when you first start in the industry. Be willing to be a passionate leader, and keep in mind the kind of the leader you had when you signed up.

Twenty years of experience has exposed me to a variety of business phases. I`ve taken countless pages of notes (including millions of mental ones) and listened to all the motivational speakers in the business. The one fact I take away from this industry is respecting the well-being of others. How you connect with them, how you treat them, what you expect, and what example you set for them. This all matters! People are always watching, analyzing, and making mental notes about you.

They see if you`re honest, willing to help when they need it, and learn your character quickly. The business realm has changed and shifted dramatically in comparison to how it was like 15 years ago. People are connecting in magnifying ways. I`ll say this, this industry is no longer about the products, it`s more about the people who have the products. It`s about those who inspire and include others in their circles of trust. When you learn to value people, they`ll learn to value you back. Make sure to be a catalyst of good ethics in this industry as technology keeps advancing.

> **Rob's Notes:** Who you become is who you`ll attract. One of the best yet most difficult parts about network marketing is that people are attracted to who you are and who you become. Be the person that treats others with respect. Be the person everyone wants around in their family, friends, church group or sports team. To put it best, sell yourself first before being a benefit to your prospect second.

Author: Tracy Rodgers

- Three years with her network marketing company.

- Team Sales $125 million dollars.

- Has 24,000 team members.

- Corporate appointed regional trainer.

- Co-author of two books.

- Founding president of the company.

- Three-time conference speaker.

- Reached the highest paid level in the compensation plan in only even months.

- Top three income earners in the entire company.

"Die with Memories,
not with Dreams"

- Rob Sperry

Rob's Notes: What Tracy doesn`t share with you is that she went from not making any money in network marketing to homeless to top earner. She went from homeless to a top earner within one year. She has one of the most powerful stories I have ever heard. I was able to watch her journey and see her massive progress. In the last two years, I have seen this woman speak LIVE in Mexico, Maui, Sundance, Utah, Canada, and Australia. This section is going to be all business and straight to the point. Learn how she recruits and closes!

Sharing The Opportunity

I`ve been involved in network marketing for over 33 years. Through the years things have changed in our industry. What`s one thing that has not changed? Building Relationships. There`s something about spending time with a group of women and bonding over the ups and downs of life, gaining confidence, and building a business.

In my 33 years of network marketing, I`ve been successful, but only to a mid-level success. I wanted so badly to be at the top level on the commission plan but never made it. I`ve discovered that there are several components to being at that top level: Passion, Sales, Recruits, and Personal Development.

Before I dive into sharing the opportunity, let`s cover passion. When you share your product, does your face light-up? Do you start talking faster and louder? Do you believe in your company`s mission, leaders, compensation plan? Do you want to tell everyone about it?

An Offer For Everyone

One amazing fact is that a side-hustle like network marketing is for everyone! The possibilities are unlimited on how far you can take your business. Our Whys & Goals are unique for each of us and are always changing, depending on needs and the growth of our business. One common comment is "I was just going to use the product myself, and before I knew it, I had a team of __". I`ve witnessed team members quit their j-o-b and be able to stay at home with their kids while their income doubles. I love to say, "Where else can you make this amount of money that`s legal, with your clothes on, standing up!"

Recruiting 101 – I like to call it Sharing the Opportunity. I`m passionate about sharing the opportunity with everyone! It doesn`t matter what they do with it; I can offer the opportunity to 10 people, all with different goals without feeling pushy or guilty because it`s about other people and not about me. If I don`t offer it when I get a chance, then I`ve made the decision to never give them the chance to hear the possibilities. I am a rock-star recruiter because I get excited for people to have the opportunity to do what I do!

Did you hear me...I said everyone? It doesn`t matter what their background is. What they look like. If they have 10 fingers and ten toes. Male. Female. Too perfect. Too shy. Strangers. Acquaintances. Where they live. How much money they make. Or don`t make it. Old. Young. Children. No children. Too busy. EVERYONE.

Being empowered to start a business and grow it has so many rewards. Team members have been able to gain confidence, get out of abusive situations, support the family when a spouse lost their job, live a life on the road giving their children an incredible experience, relieve some financial pressure, and discover what is possible for them.

This is what sharing the opportunity is all about. It`s not about making money on your commission. It`s about giving someone a chance to say yes to changing their own life. It is not my place to decide for them. If they say yes, then we can discover their vision together! This is why I love sharing the opportunity so much. There are so many amazing companies in the direct sales industry affecting so many people in the world. My goal is to change one life at a time. If I can bring happiness to one life, then we`ll have more happier children at home too.

Rob's Notes: Don`t prejudge anyone! Can you imagine someone prejudging Tracy? She hadn`t had success in network marketing in 33 years. She was homeless. She is a perfect example of why you should be willing to share your business/products with everyone.

The Fave Five

None of us want to be that pushy friend or family member that is always spamming with information overload about our business. You know when you're added to a Facebook page and then wham... you're hit with "join my team" messages. No introduction, no tell me about yourself, no back and forth chatter about life – just the Join My Team message. I bet that was not how they were approached with the business opportunity!

If you build it, they will come. Recruiting is simple once you build that relationship. So many of us want to be involved in a community. We want to have relationships. As you connect with others, they'll see your Facebook posts and the excitement you share and will get curious about what you're doing.

How my Fave Five works is simple, doable, and duplicable. Every month, you start again, and by the end of the year, that's 60 people who you've interacted with, shared a bit of life with, and either joined your team or referred someone as a team member or customer.

Let's get started! Pick five people a month that you think would be great at this business, who you'd love to work with, or who really needs something like this in their life. During the month, focus on building a relationship with them. Send voice clips (people love to hear your voice), texts, and comment on their social media posts. Let them see that you are interested in them as a person earning the know, like and trust factor. I keep a notebook close by to jot down what they're posting, pain points, and if there is any financial need, giving me insight when I do connect with them, so they know that I'm listening and genuinely care.

At the end of the month you can introduce the business and say, "This may or may not be for you, you may know someone who could use the extra money or would be great at this. I would love to give you a referral gift. Oh, and by the way, you can refer yourself." By opening with "This may or may not be for you" their wall comes down, giving them an out and opens up the conversation with them.

Close The Deal Questions

This is a game changer! Are you ready to make a change in your recruiting process? How many people do you have sitting on the fence right now? They`re interested and asked you a bunch of questions but haven`t signed up yet. In order to move forward, you have to know what it is that is holding them back. I have fine-tuned my party presentation and discovered the power of these two questions by my increased and record-breaking number of recruits through the years. Here they are:

1. "Let me ask you a question. You mentioned before that you are interested in joining my team. What is the one thing stopping you from getting a kit today and start making money next week?"

   For example, the number one objection is "I don`t have enough time." I would respond with "If I could show you how to build this business with the time you normally spend on Facebook, would you be open to that?" When I know what it is that is holding them back, I can work through it with them and they will sign-up.

2. "Hey girl, when you go to bed tonight and the first thing you are thinking about in the morning is this network marketing business, you need to get a hold of me because you need to do this. Thanks for chatting."

   I know this sounds crazy...but the two Close the Deal Questions WORK! Some people aren`t comfortable saying these at first. You have to find the words that you are comfortable saying and start practicing so you are ready to share the opportunity. One common problem we have when recruiting is that we have a lot of people who are sitting on the fence. All we need to know is the one thing that is stopping them from getting a kit and starting to make money. Once we know what that is, we can conquer the objection with them.

We are planting a seed with Question #2. Every single person will wake up and guess what thought pops into their head? Yep! You wouldn`t believe the number of team members who call me up the day after a party or after sharing the opportunity with someone and say "OMG, it works!! They signed-up!"

Know the No

We don`t have mind reading capabilities to figure out why someone doesn`t sign-up when we know the opportunity would be perfect for them. Like a Girl Scout, you need to be prepared and know what their no is...Known as the objection. Sometimes, it`s simple, like we covered above with time. It could also be they don`t know enough people, or they`re too busy.

Back in the day when we called everyone to book a party or follow-up after a party, I`d have a garbage can next to me because I`d get so nervous when working through any objection; I`d ask them to hang-on and then vomit into the garbage can. True Story! That was how nervous I was! Learning how to be comfortable out of your comfort zone is what grows you and gives you confidence. Our biggest fear is – REJECTION. I haven`t met anyone who has died because someone told them no. It`s not lethal. Just learn to not take it personally and know that it doesn`t mean no. It may mean: "Know...I need to know more" or "No...not yet."

When I`m coaching someone on my team, they may mention that they are afraid of receiving a "no" and the feeling of rejection that comes with asking a question. Think about the person at the fast food drive-thru who asks you "Do you want to super-size your meal?"... How do you think they feel when you say no? Does the employee start crying and quit because you said no? We say no all the time. Employees who are paid minimum wage are trained to ask each customer a question and no matter the answer they still continue to ask. It`s a numbers game. The more times you ask, you`ll receive no`s but then, you`ll start receiving more yeses!

The "no" changes all the time. I like to tell my team that just because it`s a "no" right now, doesn`t mean it won`t change into a "yes." I like to think of it like Thanksgiving Day. On Thanksgiving, I always say "no" to pumpkin pie when it`s first offered. I am just too stuffed to eat it right after dinner. But it`s not a "no" for very long. After resting and enjoying the day, I`m ready for that piece of pumpkin pie! I tell people just because they are full right now doesn`t mean they are going to be full in the morning. It`s important to know why they said "no" so that you can follow-up and ask again.

Rob's Notes: Tracy nailed it! Don`t be offended because someone said no. Sometimes we just need a little perspective. The fear of rejection is one of the greatest fears we all have. It ties right into the mother of all fears! The fear of judgment. Getting over yourself and these basic common fears are crucial to your success. It took me years of practice. It didn`t come naturally to me. Even after I had success, I still was very sensitive to no`s because I am a recovering people pleaser! Lol!

Rise Above

My miracle story is a testimony for how network marketing can change your life. With all my experience with different companies and positions, and my sales and recruiting skills, I ended up with a j-o-b working as a cook on our ferry system. Due to situations outside of my control, my life took a turn for the worse. After months of treading water, I found myself packing my car with four boxes and my dog. I had lost everything: my home, stability, and my security. I can`t tell you how hard this hit me. I became homeless and moved in with my mom. It was during this time that I heard about a new network marketing company that was going to be launching.

I can`t believe that all the work, failures, successes, and challenges lead me to this. I saw the vision that the new company had, and I jumped on board and shouted YES! Two months after the company launched and my business was growing, I found the book *The Game of Networking*. My business would not be where it is if I had not found Rob Sperry and his book. It was a game-changer for me!

I can`t encourage you enough to find your Passion, incorporate Personal Development daily, Learn the trade and take Action! Rob Sperry says "Successful people do the basics better!"

Author: Debbie Schneider

- Spent 25 years in the corporate world before she made the move to network marketing.

- In 2018, after 10 years in the industry, she made over 10 million dollars.

- Number seven power ranker in the world.

- During that same year she achieved the Company Vision Award.

- Team members in over eight countries.

- Received the Founder Award for recruitment, leadership, performance, and empowerment.

"Network marketing is the only industry that allows common people to earn millions with minimal investment and zero overhead, coupled with the total time freedom and joy of global travel. There are three magic words that worked for all of us who have made it to the pinnacle, and they'll work for you. they are.…."Just dont quit"

- Mark Yarnell

With or without me, this business works. I learned that from the very beginning. You have to learn to work the business and continuously grow and become better and better. Tap rooting is one strategy that can guide your business while learning how to connect and talk to prospects. In fact, this business gives anyone the opportunity to look in the mirror. I had to look in the mirror and it was with my own efforts and abilities that overcame my doubts to succeed." If it is to be... it is up to me" Anyone can learn the art of taprooting and it is really fun and creates non stop people to work with.

> **Rob's Notes:** Pay very close attention to the details in this chapter. Tap rooting is the art of sponsoring a circle of influence rather than one person. This took my recruiting strategy to another level from constant recruiting that never duplicated to only increasing my paycheck. It took me years to learn, and Debbie is one of the best I know at using it. To be candid, I spent much time with Debbie at two mastermind events in Maui and in Mexico with other top leaders present. She`s a leader of leaders and can help shave years of your financial struggles if you implement her teaching points.

Prepare to Work the Business

About 25 years into my corporate career I started seeing the writing on the wall. It was all about the numbers and everyone was just a quota and I was just a number like everyone else. Burnt out and exhausted I was looking for more, way more.. When my husband and I bought a franchise,as we thought that was the answer as so many do.... that wore us out even more. Five years of praying, working endless hours, trying to get our money back and have a future and still not the results we wanted or needed. The more money we put in, the more it took out. We finally realized this franchise wasn`t working in our favor , it was actually working against us. Time to look for other financial options to find the success I wanted but didn`t know where to look. What are our options? Along our journey, we met some very inspirational people who had changed their lives,they had gone from zero to hero with their own home business. They had amazing lifestyles, beautiful vehicles, stunning houses,and freedom, yes they were living the dream!! They were real. I thought these were just stories...fiction. And you guessed it, they were in network marketing. Why couldn`t I do this? I knew it was meant to be. I had a wake-up call, and I realized what I was missing out on. We saw their example. They were living a life that was interested in the welfare of other people. They were servant leaders and everyone worked together to achieve their desired dreams and goals. This taught me to be open in life and have a will to listen.

One of my favorite books, *The Success Principles*, got me started in network marketing. The first chapter starts out with taking ownership of your life.Chapter 1-Take 100% responsibility for your life. Every day that book was my mentor and to this day, I still go back and read. I also listened to Jim Rohn`s CDs, which I played every minute of the day and night when not building my business. I knew if I wanted to change,and grow and be successful, I needed to follow successful people. Every day for at least an hour and often much more, I would read that book. And then as I grew and continued through the journey of building this amazing business, I started reading and following other industry leaders like Rob Sperry. I learned from his story and journey and knowledge. It reminded myself my negative feelings of doubt were normal, as was the lack of confidence. Moving forward, I got stronger and stronger and more confident, my leadership grew and grew and continues today.

I didn`t have personal mentors in my life, but I did have books and training. With today`s access to the internet, anyone can find training material with a simple search. Be willing to invest in your business and find what works for you.

Sometimes, you'll struggle, and disappointments will get to you. But when you have valuable mentoring, that'll help you get over negative feelings of self-doubt. Today, I make sure I'm always filling my life with positive people, books, and training. I have done well in this amazing industry but I want to continue to grow and lead others to the endless possibilities. I spend money on my personal growth and want to be around others that lift and encourage me to grow. I really see Rob as an amazing coach and mentor for the industry and I go to his 6 and 7 figure masterminds to learn from other legends and Rob.

Find me one leader in the industry who didn't invest countless hours with mentors and teachers. Compare this to being a professional basketball player. Without the coach to teach him, the player wouldn't make it to the pros. In other words, you need to work on your personal development. The higher you go, the more you'll learn and succeed. If you let others pull you down, you'll get stuck. Continue to always prepare yourself for more education. It doesn't matter if you're brand new or a seasoned network marketer, you should always be prepared to use personal growth for more gain.

Rob's Notes: This is very significant insight. Debbie didn't have physical mentors when she started and didn't make any excuses for herself to stop. In time, she found virtual mentors. The point is, too many network marketer's make excuses about lacking mentorship rather than finding solutions. There's so many free resources available to guide you in your success. There's no excuse! Check out www.sperrybonus.com. There, you'll find the following for free on this website, *The Income Producing Activities, Your Daily Method of Operation, The Conqueror's Formula* and *Public Speaking Tips.*

Grow your Business by Growing People

The more you help people, the better leader you become and the better your business will grow. People join because of you and your leadership and what you can contribute to their lives. They don`t join just because of a product or compensation plan. They join because of your leadership and vision for the team. I started this business to change my life and to find my purpose and help others find theirs. There`s no better feeling than serving others to achieve their dreams, see their greatness, and being the best version of themselves. It just doesn`t get better than that.

I built my business organically around individuals that have never worked in this network marketing industry. I love working with people to help discover their why and to open up some of their dreams for the future. I help them get vulnerable and dig deep. It`s important to help your team get the first couple calls to get their momentum rolling. This can be one of the hardest steps, and don`t leave them now...help them get some wins, even if small. This isn`t about holding their hand; it`s about locking arms with them. You are their coach and mentor and important part of the process for them to succeed and move forward.

Our team and the culture we have created is one where everyone plays a part in helping new members and team members. Each person is important and we`re all in this together and together we grow and rise. For the first couple weeks and sometimes months, make sure to lock arms with them and help them succeed. They need some wins, large and small. Now don`t get the idea that we drag and pull people but we "run or walk the same speed as you". We match the energy of the team member. There is a place for everyone. Some people here just for the products and some for the culture and amazing people, they are an important part of the team also . And we put them " in the soup"...the regular training and events. But builders that want to build? We go with a huge sense of urgency. Success loves speed.

To become a top earner, you have to stop caring about what others think. People thought I was crazy, and some still do, but that doesn`t matter to me. What matters are my core values of empowering others to be their best and inspiring them to step up and lead. People will have their opinions about you before you start network marketing and have them afterward, too. Who cares? Let your actions do the talking. In fact, I had to change the people who I hung out with. I didn`t realize how important it was to surround myself with other like-minded people. The friends I have now are amazing. We push, uplift, inspire, and make each other want to be better people and leaders.

Rob's Notes: Here comes the tap rooting section. Take some crazy notes here!

Tap Rooting

I have helped bring in thousands of people into my organization though tap rooting. What defines tap rooting is supporting people who want to grow individually and on a team. For example, let's take a lemon. Tap rooting is when you get the most juice out of the lemon. You're utilizing the team and who they know through who they know.

Always ask them who they know . Let's say a team member invites ten people they met at the library or concert to the next meeting. Out of those ten, only two are interested, but you see we now have two people. We start the same process with those two, asking them who they know. This is the art of duplicating your business. Keep creating repetition in your recruiting strategy to increase team volume. You never run out of people to work with and build the business.

 I work with all my teams and lines in my organization and of course depends on the strength of the leadership in those lines. There's never a line in my organization where I don't provide support too but of course at different levels. If there's someone ten or twenty levels down and they're running, and need help, I run with them. Side note- always ensuring to not overstep if amazing leadership is already there doing the job, I just cheer on. If they need help or want to push harder, I'm here for guidance. This creates an amazing culture of support and leadership.

Working with leaders is also valuable because everyone wins. During my ten years of using tap rooting, my leadership skills became more effective. Now, many times I find not needed at all.We have built amazing leaders that are duplicating the taprooting to its fullest..." .
So guess what I get to do....and other leaders, go share this amazing

opportunity with others and continue to grow the team. This is the concept of tap rooting and duplication.

You never know what someone can be capable of and my job is to pull out their greatness.With tap rooting we have had huge success in the world thru the amazing leaders and teams in my organization and because of that have changed many lives with the products, the culture and the opportunity.We have created people who get the products for free, some who make $500 a month for their vacation fun money, some who make $5000 a month and changed their career, and some who have made 6 and 7 figures and have become millionaires and legends in this industry. Honestly, this wouldn`t have happened if my team didn`t consistently tap root through members and their prospects. When you learn how to do this, your marketing methods become more productive. A great tip is I always have one person sitting next to me learning how to tap root while another teaches it to our team .Duplicate and teach taprooting and your business will be so strong and always moving forward.

Anywhere, Anyone

Persistent back to back events is a huge deal. I don`t care if it is a coffee date, a regional event, a three-way messenger group, or a zoom call. I like to do them all as it keeps the environment creative, exciting and fun. Tap rooting plays a vital role in any business atmosphere.

The best aspects about global events are the relationships you develop with new team members. Planned out, I`d go to a specific city and basically move in. I`d sleep on apartment floors, couches, wherever I could. In Vancouver BC, on the first day of the event, myself and my leaders would give one to seven presentations. The crowds and people walking around motivated me as well as all the others.Energy creates energy. Tap rooting makes the whole process very exciting. Sometimes, we as leaders get feedback from others who worry this business will burn them out, but it`s the exact opposite. Progress and mometunem in the business provides thrilling amounts of energy and it doesn`t feel like work. After meeting people all day long in presentation after presentation as the first 10 people would go tell their friends and they would come to hear thru the day, we would end the day with a final presentation in the hotel room. After that, we left it up for them to decide if they wanted to join us or not and it was their choice to make.But the excitement of the taprooting and duplication is so powerful and they could feel the energy also and it is hard to walk away from that energy. It`s amazing to see how tap rooting led me and my leaders to new cities, new people, new teams, and new countries. In all of these countries, I have met some extraordinary people who now are top leaders changing lives everyday.

The key to growing internationally is a willingness to travel and spending lots of time in the countries you want to grow in and doing crazy hours on your computer...while your family sleeps. Yes, I have used zoom webinars for years and built amazing teams but there will be the time you need to go to those areas as belly to belly is so key in building relationships and trust and teamwork . Learn the skill of tap rooting, go out, and teach it. It will amplify your network!

Ask for referrals..... I was at an appointment with a businessman who I thought this opportunity would be so amazing for him and with his skills and lifestyle. . He said no, but he knew two ladies who were looking for opportunities like this. Long story short, after meeting these gogetter women and tap rooting them, we built a beautiful strong business that is still building today. Always ask for referrals as you never know who they know. So often we feel, "am I being pushy? Not at all. My first contact for a major team in a new country that was opening...made one call with us to a potential prospect and that was a beginning to a beautiful large team. That individual ended up quitting as the business was not for her but because we taprooted , the duplication continued for many many levels and still does.

Your mindset is key and you will always have negative thoughts in your mind...and big hint...don`t keep them long in your mind. It really is your choice how you think and we get to choose our success. Go right back to your personal growth and your mentors and what are you reading and listening to.

To be of more value, I believe where you focus your energy will be the main strength of your team. If your energy is about winning, then your team will radiate that from you. This is similar to the analogy of starting a fire and letting it rise.

Carry the torch and others will follow. At times, your team may be stagnant, but the more you tap root, the more business it´ll bring to your network. It will not only furnish the team with more productive energy but offer movement and warmth which lets the fire stay lit. That´s why tap rooting is essential. At the end of the day, it extracts more prospects that have been waiting for opportunities like this to join your network.

As mentioned, tap rooting is time efficient and can work in your favor. When team members master this skill, they become their own leaders while recruiting new members. The benefits are that your team grows, allowing you to invest your time in other parts of your business that need attention and growth. For you, this can be traveling the world attending seminars, buying materials for your next event, taking the team out to a sporting event, and paying for lead advertising on Facebook. Everyone wins, and you are on-autopilot while they run your business. One way or another, the flame stays lit for good.

Give Vision

Keep in mind you have a story from day one. Act as if you paid $500,000 to start your network marketing business. Because guess what? You`ll show up, you can do this, and it`ll change your life! Good leaders have vision, but great leaders give vision. Paint the picture all the time. What does the movie of your life look like? What does the movie of your business look like?

I say this to myself every day, "with or without me, this business works." It`s not the business or the company that isn`t working, it`s you. People are addicted to average. You have to be willing to sacrifice whatever it takes. My friend told me she would rather be watching "The Bachelor" every Monday night than work. Giving up old hobbies, going to the movies, or watching tv are what I gave up to spend time on upscaling my business. Sometimes people say, "I can`t make it to a meeting tonight because 'Survivor is on.`" I always think, "well geez, how are you going to survive?" Why watch the world series on tv when you can go to the world series. Go back and paint the picture. Be the one to show the vision as a leader. Let others see what`s possible to gain from making better choices.

Some say I was lucky since I got in the company when it launched. After all these years, I know several people who`re still with the company and many those who left. This is why having your own vision is important. I can`t stress it enough. If you don`t want it, then you`ll never have it. There are days when I don`t want to get out of bed and take action on my business. But it`s my vision that keeps me going. It`s so strong that when I do get out of bed I say, "I have got today. I am going to go and change lives." These affirmations thrill me with excitement! As you work on your vision, over time it`ll grow and become more meaningful. Mine has grown and continues to change, but you always have to be conscious of it. You see, I don`t need anyone motivating me since that`s what my vision is for. There are people that stumble upon trying to figure out their vision. When this happens, teach them to dream, be their visionary, and paint a picture that magnifies their inspiration and success. Even when I was making $500 a month, I still painted the picture for myself.

Keep going and lock arms, dive into people`s contacts, see who they know that wants in on this action, and help them overcome their fears. With all honesty, I don`t believe you can have a strong business without tap rooting. Don`t miss out on valuable people by using this strategy! Honestly, I don`t know how you can move forward in business without it. Friends know more people than they think. Make sure to utilize those skill sets to expand your network and bring those 10 people on board! You never know who you`ll find. Sometimes you may enroll one friend who does very little to bring their sister on board who does what they can to bring their father on board who then becomes that superstar you`re looking for. Keep tap rooting and dig through those contacts!And see you at the top....I can`t wait to hear your story!!!

CONCLUSION

"The common denominator of success – the secret of success of everyone who has ever been successful lies in the fact that the person formed the habit of doing things that others don't like to do. It's just as true as it sounds and it's just as simple as it seems."

- Albert Gray

Become the type of person you want to recruit. In reality, the only person you`re going to recruit is yourself. Think about it. If you truly recruit yourself, it`s not a question of "if," but of "when." It`s true that your members will help you grow your team, but don`t get into management mode thinking they`re the ones doing the work.

You have to keep recruiting and set the example. You`re the leader. The authors in this book exemplify how they became experts in recruiting. They`re all top leaders and recruiters because they keep the foundation for business the same. They recruit and work on their skills, and are always being a leader AND a recruiter.

After reading this book, I want you to ask yourself these questions,

> "Am I implementing these recruiting tips and systems into my business?"

> "Am I teaching my team how to implement these tips and systems into their businesses?"

What matters most is taking action on your business. Use what you learned from these amazing authors to become a great recruiter. Take time, effort, and due diligence to become a great leader. See what`s important and forecast the vision for your future. To learn more about what it takes to bring your skills up to the next level, visit www.sperrybonus.com.

A special thanks goes out to all the amazing authors in this book. You inspire me daily. You`re always pushing me to learn and grow. You`re the reason I get to do what I do every day...and for that... I`m eternally in your debt and grateful to you.

Your friend,

Rob Sperry

CPSIA information can be obtained
at www.ICGtesting.com
Printed in the USA
LVHW022303200720
661166LV00019B/2787